PURPLE SQUIRREL

Stand Out, Land Interviews, and Master the Modern Job Market

MICHAEL B. JUNGE

ISBN-10: 1467992607

EAN-13: 9781467992602

Library of Congress Control Number: 2010911539

CreateSpace, North Charleston, SC

PRAISE FOR *PURPLE SQUIRREL*

"Insightful, optimistic, and practical. A great resource for the 21st century job seeker." Mary Hamershock, Director of People Operations, Google

"The best job seeker and career book in decades - an almost unfair advantage in the modern job market." Archie Holton, CEO Odyssey Seminars

"An insightful and practical guide to mastering the job search process." Sophie Beaurpere, Director of Communications at Indeed.com

An engaging, well-written, and comprehensive guide to getting ahead in the 21st century job market. Dr. Paul Powers, Author of *Winning Job Interviews* and *Love Your Job*

"Mike Junge is one of the most thorough and knowledgeable recruiters in the country, and his insight into job search is something you're unlikely to find anywhere else in the marketplace. In this book, he breaks down each aspect of the hiring process so you get a full understanding of today's changing job market and the tools required to master it. *Purple Squirrel* will give you an edge over your competition and help you move your career forward at a pace you never thought possible. This is a must read for anyone looking at their next career move!" Michael D. Ellis, President and Co-Founder Surrex Solutions Corporation

"Given the current economic challenges and the highly competitive nature of today's difficult marketplace, *Purple Squirrel* is the right book at the right time. Junge provides a practical, workable approach that includes inspiration, perspective, and purposeful planning. The reader will be effectively equipped with the tools to not only land a job, but, even more valuable, Junge provides a current, relevant and effective road map to a successful life and a healthy financial future. I highly recommend it." Jay Heinlein, Published Media and Marketing Professional

"This is a book for everyone…it empowers the reader to build their own roadmap to success by helping them definitively determine where they are now, and where they truly want to go. The number of 'I never thought of it that way, but that's brilliant' moments in this book is astounding! I will use this book not only in my own life, and also to help my clients as a recruiter, career coach and executive mentor." Joe Diersing, Director of Staffing and Placement, NexGen Consultants

"After ten years of experience recruiting for Fortune 100 companies and start-ups, I can say with confidence that the material in *Purple Squirrel* holds true in the real world. It is the new play book for professional success, and an effective guide for managing the achievement of your goals. It's not just about getting the next job but building your career, and *Purple Squirrel* offers sound advice to practice." Mike Walsh, R&D Recruiter, VMware

"A powerful, practical, and entertaining read. *Purple Squirrel* may be the first innovative job seeker book that truly makes sense for the technology age. As a business owner, I hope anyone who interviews with us takes most, if not all, of Junge's advice." Gini Dietrich, Chief Executive Officer at Arment Dietrich, author of *Spin Sucks* (www.spinsucks.com)

"*Purple Squirrel* is both advanced and basic - it really nails some of the fundamentals that could be considered the secrets of "the lucky people." Mike does a brilliant job of giving not only the how to's - step by step - but also the why behind the process. You walk away feeling like "now I get it!" ~ Linda Rouyer, Entrepreneur

"Michael Junge sets the standard for professional excellence in the recruiting industry. He knows the employment world inside and out and has successfully guided countless job seekers through the hiring process. With this book, Michael shares his secrets and provides a step by step approach to getting ahead and achieving life and career goals in the real world. I highly recommend *Purple Squirrel* for anyone looking to advance their career or land the job of their dreams." ~ Perry Deschamps, Executive Recruiter and Account Manager

"Michael Junge has truly captured the dynamic and ever-changing job market. His insight and expertise will allow job seekers to take their careers to the next level and maximize search strategies to achieve success." ~ Debra Wheatman, CPRW, CPCC, President, Careers Done Write (www.careersdonewrite.com)

"*Purple Squirrel* is a valuable and practical read…a must-have for modern job seekers." ~ Sandy Laskin, Vice President, Information Technology at Stonewater Staffing

"With this book, having the job you want seems obtainable. As a soon-to-be graduate, having this blueprint will be exceptionally beneficial in keeping me ahead of my fellow graduates. This book is not only helpful to those already familiar with the job market, but also those who are eager to enter it." ~ Anne Pearson, Student at Xavier University and Intern at Procter & Gamble

ACKNOWLEDGEMENTS

Bringing *Purple Squirrel* to life has been a labor of love, and I feel profoundly grateful to the countless people who contributed to the success of this project. Special thanks to my family – Mom, Dad, Amy, Mikey, Emma, Brenton, Justin, Kevin, PJ, and all of the fantastic in-laws – I couldn't ask for a better system of love, support, and brilliance. To my coaches and mentors – Shrfu, Archie, Tony, Mike, Joe, Glenn, Ram, Randy, Betsy, Bob, Lou, Rich, Michele, and many more – thanks for being extraordinary! To great friends – past, present and future – my life is far richer for knowing you. A super big bonus thanks to Justin Junge, Amy Junge, Richard Bolles, and Sue-Ellen Fox for going above and beyond in their contributions to this book.

You are all loved and appreciated!
Mike

TABLE OF CONTENTS

LETTER TO THE READER

PART I: A FOUNDATION FOR SUCCESS

PART II: BECOMING AN OPPORTUNITY MAGNET

PART III: GETTING ON THE FAST TRACK

FINAL THOUGHTS

Dear Reader,

The fact that you've picked up this book (or clicked on it) indicates that you're in a job search now or expect to be in the relatively near future. In either case, you probably have a lot on your mind. What's next for me? What are my options? Can I find a great job in the current economy? Can I find a new job at all? Is it possible to do something I deeply enjoy and still earn the kind of living I want? Can I take it to the next level and thrive financially while doing something I absolutely love?

Sorting your way through those questions is a big enough challenge, but in reality you're facing a lot of others as well. The modern job market is complex and fast-moving. If you don't understand what employers are searching for *today* - or where, how, and why they go hunting for talent - your job search and career are in for a very bumpy ride.

Globalization, recession, job boards, search engines, and online networking sites have opened the world to an almost unlimited supply of resources. There are literally hundreds of millions of resumes and career profiles available for review at any given point in time. Add in the high volume of online applicants, and it's easy to see why most job seekers struggle to attract attention from motivated employers.

Ironically, employers are struggling on the other side of the exact same equation – sorting through the sheer volume of potential applicants and zeroing in on a much smaller field of high-probability candidates. As a result, job descriptions tend to be overburdened and resume searches confined to prohibitively specific criteria. Everyone seems to be looking for an almost impossible mix of qualifications, skills and experiences. In the staffing industry, we call this "searching for purple squirrels."

As a job seeker and professional, one of your primary goals should be getting to the place where you are readily identified as such a resource. To that end, this book is designed as a personal mentor and guide. Drawing on insight and wisdom of some of the best executives, career coaches, and recruiters in the business world, *Purple Squirrel* will help you navigate the changing marketplace and position yourself for extraordinary success – both now and in the future.

As you move into the main text, there are a few ideas and concepts to which I'd like to draw your attention. First is the layout of the book itself, which is designed with a deliberate structure and progression. You'll find the material in the second and third sections far more effective when layered on the foundation created in the first, so even though you may want to skip forward to a particular section or topic – I recommend that you don't. If you start at the beginning and work your way through Part I, the rest of the content will prove far more valuable and effective.

Next is the idea of a Fast Tracker. For the purposes of this book, a Fast Tracker is someone who lands great jobs and accelerates their way up the corporate ladder as a result of intelligent strategy and outstanding performance (as opposed to politicking, game play, or ethical compromise). Many chapters and sub-sections of this book contain Fast Track Challenges. These are exercises designed to put your search and career on an increasingly upward trajectory and should be taken on as an integral part of the process.

Last is the goal of becoming an Opportunity Magnet. The job market may be complex and full of challenges, but it is equally full of powerful tools and resources for attracting the attention of prospective employers. Transforming yourself into an Opportunity Magnet is about combining modern tools with effective preparation and performance so that great opportunities come looking for you. That's the real purpose of this book – to guide you to the point where you can stop being a job seeker and start being a sought-after resource. Regardless of how distant that idea may sound right now, it is absolutely possible and well within your grasp.

With optimism and appreciation,
Mike

PART I
A Foundation for Success

A GOOD PLACE TO START

"You get in life what you have the courage to ask for."

Oprah Winfrey

❦

I was a nineteen-year-old sophomore at the University of Arizona when my dad handed me a copy of Anthony Robbins' *Awaken the Giant Within*. The title was intriguing. The possibility that I might have enormous potential was flat-out exhilarating. If I happened to possess any latent talents and innate abilities I wanted to tap into them, and I wanted to do it as fast as humanly possible. I picked the book up and started reading.

Within pages I was hooked. Tony's stories of personal success inspired me to think and believe bigger than I ever had. Schoolwork and required reading got shuffled to the side and I jumped into the book full speed. I bought a lined yellow notepad, scrawled the words "Personal Development Workbook" across the top, and proceeded to write out the goals, vision, and thoughts that showed up as I worked my way through each chapter.

The process was hugely empowering, and by the time I finished the last page I felt ready to go out and conquer the world. Unfortunately, my attention span was less than stellar. Within weeks of finishing the last page I set the book aside and moved on to more pressing activities. The vision and goals would come to mind on occasion, but my attention was on girls, friends, parties, and school (in roughly that order). Eventually the little yellow notebook went into storage and the memory of what I'd envisioned faded into the background of the overall college experience.

Almost a decade later, as my wife and I moved into our new house in Irvine, my parents stopped by to unload half a dozen boxes of my old stuff. Apparently being a homeowner meant they were no longer obliged to store the accumulated remnants of my childhood, and they couldn't have been more pleased. Feeling somewhat indignant, I moved everything into the garage and started digging through my things.

As I sorted through the boxes, deciding what to keep and what to throw away, I stumbled across the little yellow notebook. It had been years since I'd last seen it, but as I flipped the pages an unexpected and undeniable truth stared me square in the face. Without conscious effort or willful intent I had achieved the vast majority of the goals I'd set for myself ten years earlier.

There were exceptions, of course. I still didn't have a Ferrari, helicopter, or private island, and my grasp of French was remedial at best, but almost everything I'd written down had been accomplished. I'd learned to speak fluent Spanish, met and married an extraordinary woman, traveled the world, published poetry, become a six-figure executive, earned a black belt, founded a startup, bought a home, and helped build a nationwide staffing company. I was in awe. How was it possible to have accomplished so many of my goals while putting so little attention into the process?

It didn't make sense, but the experience of creating a vision and defining my goals had obviously been more powerful than previously imagined. *Awaken the Giant Within* became mandatory reading for the recruiters and sales people in my training programs, joining *The Seven Habits of Highly Effective People* and *Influence: The Psychology of Persuasion* (all highly recommended).

This book starts with a similar focus because it is vitally important to define what you're hoping to get out of the job market **before** attempting to master it. Landing a job can be about survival, or it can be a pathway to fulfillment, purpose, and financial freedom. Among other things, this book is about empowering you to take the latter path.

As you read forward, you might want to grab a little yellow notebook of your own. Getting ideas down on paper has a particular magic to it, especially when it comes to defining the things you want to create in life. It's also pretty cool to think that one day you might dig up documented proof that you set out to do something amazing and totally kicked butt at making it happen.

A FOUNDATION FOR SUCCESS

Architects and structural engineers understand that the scale to which a structure can be built depends on the strength of the foundation on which it will be supported. A skyscraper requires a foundation with depth proportional to its height, and the same is true in every other area of life.

The foundation for a career is comprised of countless elements, ranging from innate gifts and talents to education, experience, skills, socio-economics, upbringing, and personal connections. Some of these factors can be influenced or changed, and others can't. For the purposes of this book, we'll be focusing only on those things that can be impacted right now, today, or sometime in the immediate future. Anything outside your scope of control will simply be put to the side and ignored, at least for now.

THE POWER OF MINDSET

"Nothing can stop the man with the right mental attitude from achieving his goal; nothing on earth can help the man with the wrong mental attitude."

W.W. Ziege

Yogi Berra was a hall-of-fame baseball player and manager, but is most often remembered for cleverly abusing the English language. His famous quote, "Ninety percent of the game is half mental," was considered amusing at the time, but is now recognized as a striking understatement. One could very well say that one hundred percent of success in life is ninety nine percent mental.

Air Force Colonel George Hall is a prime example of this principle. In the early 1960s he was a talented pilot and an ordinary golfer. His best round was nowhere near scratch, but he enjoyed getting out on the links as much as anything other than flying and time with family.

When he found himself locked up in a North Vietnamese Prisoner of War camp in 1965, his passion for golf become something much more powerful. Called actively into memory and imagination, golf became a lifeline to home and to the future.

For seven years, as Colonel Hall lived in almost unimaginable conditions, he visualized himself playing round after round of golf. He played each hole, each club selection, and each shot exactly as if he were out on the links in person. He practiced his favorite course in his mind over and over and over, until every square inch was indelibly etched into his imagination. Not long after being rescued and brought home in 1973, Colonel Hall returned to play a round at the course he'd imagined most frequently during his imprisonment. When he did, something unexpectedly incredible happened – he shot a 76, the best round of his life.[1]

Instead of focusing on all of the countless things he couldn't change, Colonel Hall focused on two things he could control – his mindset and imagination. As a result, he discovered a secret of success recognized by countless top athletes, executives, coaches, and entrepreneurs alike – that a positive and focused mind has the power to move mountains and make the seemingly impossible happen (often in completely unpredictable ways).

For many people, work is a form of imprisonment every bit as real as a jail cell or prison camp. A job is seen as an unavoidable and unpleasant fact of life, something that must be done no matter what, regardless of how painful or uninspiring it might be. Individuals such as Colonel Hall show

---

1   http://www.pownetwork.org/bios/h/h075.htm; *The Winner's Edge*, Denis Waitley, Berkley Books

that physical bonds can be transcended by mental inventiveness. Relatively speaking, breaking free from a disempowered outlook is pretty simple. Work doesn't have to be a form of servitude. With the right attitude, it can be much, much more.

If you're willing to improve your attitude, a good place to start is with a simple reality check. As a mentor once counseled me, you can always figure out what's going on in your mind by looking at the results you're experiencing in reality. A simple process for figuring it out is to 1) Look closely at the results that you are producing, and 2) Evaluate the mindset and thought patterns that led to those results.

Take a moment right now and think about where you are in your career. Are you happy with what you see? Do you like your current or most recent job? Is it rewarding and fulfilling (or was it)? Are you achieving all of the success you know to be possible? Spend a minute describing where you currently are and how the results stack up with your expectations of yourself. Be brutally honest, and write down whatever shows up for you.

WHERE I AM NOW:

If you're feeling fully satisfied with your life and career, the mindset that got you to this point is owed a great big thank you. If not, your thinking probably requires some fine tuning. Either way it's useful to identify the thought patterns behind the results in your life, and there are ALWAYS patterns hiding behind the results in your life. Usually you'll find at least a few that aren't empowering, and often the dominant thoughts will directly interfere with your ability to perform at the highest level possible.

Take a moment to think about how you relate to work. How do you describe your job to someone you are meeting for the very first time? What do you say when you talk to friends about your day to day business? What's your immediate reaction to waking up on a given Monday and knowing you have to go to the office? Complete each of the following sentences with the first word or phrase that pops into your mind. If you're currently out of work, think about your most recent job as you go through this exercise.

Work is a/an _____

On Monday morning when I'm on my way to the office I feel _____

My favorite part of the work week is_____

My job _____

I wish I_____

What specific words, thoughts, and feelings show up? What happens when you think about walking into the office first thing in the morning? Do you relate to your job as an opportunity or a pain in the neck? Is work something you "have to do" or something you "want to do?" Is it a necessary evil or a pathway for contribution and personal fulfillment? Do you love what you do, or do you wish you could quit and never go back again?

If "work sucks" and you "have to" go to a "J-O-B" where you grit your teeth and spend the week waiting for 5 p.m. on Friday, eventually you're going down. Someone is going to outwork, outsmart, outhustle, outperform, and otherwise leave you standing in their dust. They'll be on their way to promotions while you're holding a stack of papers and muttering about your lame boss, crappy job, and all the work you "have to" do. That's if you're lucky. The other alternative is that your skill set becomes outdated, undervalued, or obsolete, in which case you'll be replaced, downsized, outsourced, off-shored, or just plain fired.

The global marketplace and emergence of resume search engines has opened the door to a significantly larger talent pool. You're no longer competing with comparably skilled resources in just your local market—you're fighting for your next job with people on entirely different continents who would be thrilled to get the work at 40-50 percent of your current salary (if not less). How do you compete in a market like that?

For starters, you have to let go of any sense of *entitlement* you might have relating to your income and career. Employment isn't a right. Nobody owes you a job or a paycheck. Not current or past employers, not the people you meet on interviews, and certainly not the government. Jobs and compensation have to be earned through the fair exchange of value. That's the way a free market yields rewards to those who actively contribute and punishes those less willing to make a difference.

Next, you have to be someone that others WANT to work with. People want to work with individuals who enjoy what they do, have a positive attitude, and are willing to lend a helping hand. Even if you are highly skilled and talented, a negative attitude or disruptive personality will eventually lead to the unemployment line. You have to get along with your customers, leaders, and peers. The more you enjoy what you do, the easier that becomes.

Last, and most importantly, you have to BE WORTH IT. If you want to avoid outsourcing, downsizing, replacement, and firing, you have to perform at a level that makes the cost of losing you greater than anything that might be gained by letting you go. The more knowledgeable, skilled, and valuable you become, the more secure your job and future will be. You become valuable by understanding the goals of others (particularly customers, managers, and employers), contributing to the achievement of those goals, and constantly developing and expanding your own skills and abilities.

A key to achieving all three is to adopt a mindset of opportunity. That means making an intentional effort to look for the hidden upside in everything you face in life—from the most mundane and ordinary of tasks to the most challenging and problematic of situations.

If "mindset of opportunity" doesn't feel quite right for you, find a different word or phrase that does (consider "solutions oriented," "value focused," "unstoppable," or something similar). Define it however you wish, but make sure the words you use strike a chord. An adopted mindset has to feel right if it's going to make a difference, so it's a good idea to experiment until you come up with something that rings true. Write down a few possibilities here, and then pick the one that lights you up.

POSSIBLE MINDSETS:

The mindset I am adopting is _____

Now, focusing on your new mindset, repeat the exercise from the beginning of this chapter.

Work is a/an _____

On Monday morning when I'm on my way to the office I feel _____

My favorite part of the work week is _____

My job _____

I wish I _____

Did your responses feel better the second time around? If they did, you're on the right track. If not, take some more time to come up with something that inspires a more optimistic outlook. When you've found a word or phrase that empowers a great attitude, write it on a separate piece of paper and put that paper in a place where you can see it daily (e.g. taped to a computer monitor, mirror or wallet). Remind yourself of this new mindset as often as possible – it will serve as fuel for outstanding performance and a safeguard against extended bouts of negativity.

CREATING A VISION FOR LIFE

"The best way to predict the future is to create it."

Peter Drucker

✿ ✿ ✿

In 1927 Buckminster Fuller was flat broke, literally penniless. To make matters worse, he had a family that depended on him, and no earthly idea of how to provide for them. In a period of intense despair, he set out to solve his problem the only way he could imagine – by jumping off a bridge and ending his life. As he stood ready to leap into the freezing water below, a thought entered his mind that significantly altered the course of his future. The thought was "to see what a penniless, unknown human individual with a dependent wife and newborn child might be able to do effectively on behalf of all humanity..."[2]

Had Buckminster gone on to a mundane or ordinary life, his decision to live would have been unlikely to enter the history books (though still right and brave). Fortunately, that's not what happened. Far from it. For the next fifty-five years, Buckminster "Bucky" Fuller lived an extraordinary life, becoming one of America's most influential figures and contributing profoundly in numerous fields of endeavor. He left a lasting impact in the areas of architecture and philosophy, coined the famously clever phrase "Spaceship Earth," and was the creator of the Geodesic dome. He designed the Montreal Biosphere, authored numerous books and publications, and pioneered the field of Synergetics.

---

2   Buckminster Fuller, Grunch of Giants, 1983, and a first hand account by someone who knew Bucky personally

Over the course of his life, Bucky influenced the thinking of countless political leaders, scientists, and prominent members of society. He made numerous innovations in the area of low-cost structures and housing, and left behind a legacy that continues to impact the world we live in today.

When asked, Bucky would insist that he wasn't a genius, that he was no more brilliant than many other human beings. He would claim that he was just a guy who started out with absolutely nothing and was willing to do whatever he could to make a positive contribution. In the end, it wasn't talent or IQ that made the difference – it was a willingness to step into a larger vision and the courage to take consistent action toward making it happen.

As you look at your career and future, you may not see a vision as inspiring and compelling as the one Bucky created. Then again, you're probably not standing on the edge of a bridge with absolutely nothing to lose (and that's a good thing). You don't have to push yourself to the brink to find purpose, and you don't have to take on a vision that requires changing the world in order to feel happy and satisfied.

That being said, if you're going to create a vision, you might as well dream up something bigger than "paying the bills." While you're at it, consider aiming for something that actively inspires you. After all, if you're going to spend the next few decades of your life as a working professional, you might as well have something worth working for.

Vision is one of the keys to sustaining a positive attitude, and attitude is one of the keys to success as both a job seeker and working professional. Regardless of how talented you may be, or how inspired you are right now, work will eventually show up as a burden. It just will. When that happens, a sense of purpose will help you stay in action and sustain a positive attitude, even on the days when that's not how you feel and not what you want to do.

Like it or not, attitude projects through every aspect of your job search *and* on-the-job performance. It influences the decisions of those with whom you work, those who would consider hiring you, and those in a position to impact your career in a positive or negative direction. It shapes your day-to-day performance, affects the people around you, and changes the quality of results you produce. The better your attitude, the better your career prospects – and vice versa.

When your attitude projects anything other than confidence, passion, focus, and purpose, you do yourself a huge disservice. Those in a position to hire or help you toward a dream job may not be able to put their finger on exactly why, but something about you will raise red flags and make them uneasy about having you on their team. They may like you. They may feel you are qualified and capable. They probably won't hire or promote you.

People are drawn to passion and energy, so it's no surprise that one of the keys to landing *great* job opportunities is projecting genuine enthusiasm and appreciation for what you do. Ordinary people land ordinary jobs. Passionate people land extraordinary jobs. Passion is generated by enjoying your work and feeling inspired by what you do or what your work empowers. This happens effortlessly when you experience work as a reflection and expression of who you are, and is all but impossible otherwise.

BEGINNING AT THE END

In *The Seven Habits of Highly Effective People,* Steven Covey has his readers put life in perspective by imagining themselves at their own funeral, much like Ebenezer Scrooge chaperoned by the ghost of Christmas future. He asks his audience to think about who will speak at their funeral – friends, family, and community members – and what these people will say. The exercise is profoundly impactful and helps put present issues and challenges into a whole new perspective.

This next section provides an opportunity to take advantage of the same principal, with a few subtle twists thrown in. Even if you've done something similar in the past, allow yourself to engage fully in the experience as if it were the first time. You're a different person today than you were last year, last week, and last chapter. Give yourself the freedom to explore who you are TODAY and where you are committed to going tomorrow and into the future.

YOUR FUNERAL

Imagine for a moment that you are at your own funeral, observing from a viewpoint that allows you to see and hear all that is occurring around you. Imagine further that you have a complete and perfect view of the entire journey of your life, start to finish.

From this semi-omniscient perspective, read each question, close your eyes and notice what shows up. Take in as much of the experience as you can, in as much detail as you can. When you've done that, come back to the questions and write down your thoughts and impressions in the space below or in your own notebook.

Be honest with the details about who you are, who you've become, and what you want to leave behind when you move on from this world. If you don't like what you see, consider this an opportunity to rewrite the script. Be true to yourself and the person you wish to become. If you think big and play hard, you just might get there.

- Who am I? What kind of person have I become?

- What have I accomplished and experienced in my life?

- What have I contributed to the world and people around me?

- What impact has career had on my life as a whole?

- Who are the three people I most want to hear say they are proud of me? Why?

- What do I most want to be able to say about myself and the life I have lived?

FAST TRACK CHALLENGE:

Reread the details of what you have just written. Let the vision sink in and impact you at a fundamental level, then take a few minutes to rewrite and summarize the key points.

My Vision for the Future:

ZOOMING IN

"You have to find something that you love enough to be able to take risks, jump over the hurdles and break through the brick walls that are always going to be placed in front of you. If you don't have that kind of feeling for what it is you're doing, you'll stop at the first giant hurdle."

George Lucas

Having created a vision for life as a whole, the next step is to get a little more granular and create a vision for your career. Although the context of your professional life isn't as broad or all-encompassing as the first, the two should be congruent. Your vision for life should inform and empower your career track, and your day to day work should move you in the direction of your overall goals.

The following exercise is a great deal like the last, only this time the setting is your retirement dinner. This could be the day you sell your last business, formally retire from the corporate world, or otherwise step away from the ranks of the officially employed—whichever best fits your vision for the future. Just as in the first exercise, read the questions first, then close your eyes and imagine the experience before writing down your answers. Once you've done that, come back and document what you see.

- What career or profession did I choose? Why?

- How has my career contributed to fulfilling my greater vision for life?

- What have I contributed to the world through my career? What difference have I made for others?

- Who is at my retirement dinner? Why did they come, and what will they say about me?

- What will be my parting message to those around me? What advice will I give to my family and friends as they move forward in their own lives?

What did you see? Are you inspired by what you just created? Does your current career have you on target to achieve this vision? If you're already on track, great! You have just affirmed one the most important choices you'll make in your adult life and can move forward with confidence and upward focus. If not, this is a great opportunity to shift viewpoints, reflect, and discover what it will take to get on track.

Either way, write down at least three distinct professions that could allow you to reach the end of your career feeling satisfied and fulfilled. Even if you love what you do right now, it's a good exercise to consider alternatives that could produce similar feelings of contribution and satisfaction. Life can be funny at times, and it never hurts to have a backup plan (or two). You can, of course, include what you're currently doing as one of the three alternatives.

1) _____

2) _____

3) _____

Which is your favorite? Do a quick check and see if what you have written is a legitimate career path or a hobby. If you're unclear, a hobby is something you deeply enjoy but is highly unlikely to generate a livable income. A career should incorporate one or more aspects of what makes the hobby enjoyable and also meets the additional criteria of being able to provide a sustainable income. Income, along with a tangible benefit to a specific community, is ultimately what differentiates a career from a hobby.

Of the career paths you listed, pick the one that best fits the criteria for a viable profession and most lights you up. As mentioned above, the requirements for a proper vocation include the ability to generate consistent income, congruence with personal goals and vision, and a benefit to at least one outside community. Write your favorite here.

My Ideal Career: _____

The next step is to figure out what it will take to move you in the direction of your target profession. Will it require specialized training, certification, or formal education? Is it something you can take on part-time to begin with? What tools, resources, skills, and experience will you need to build in order to successfully move in this direction? Start thinking about what it will take to get on track, and use the next several sections to create a plan for making it happen.

FAST TRACK CHALLENGE:

Identify at least one action that can move you in the direction of your desired career path, and take it.

DEFINING YOUR LONG-TERM GOALS

Now that you have a vision for the "end game" and a specific career in mind, the next step is to translate what you've envisioned into clear, tangible, long-term goals. Setting long-term goals is a great way to gain perspective and remind yourself how much life and career you still have in front of you. In ten years you can earn a doctorate degree, build a business (or business empire), change career tracks, fund a charitable organization, and much, much more.

As you create your long-term goals, don't limit your imagination or ambition. You aren't going to achieve everything you want to accomplish right away, but if you take consistent action—even a few minutes a day—you can achieve extraordinary things over the course of a decade. The act of writing these goals will help you unlock and harness your innate energy and power, and will set in motion events and opportunities far beyond the scope of imagination.

As you start writing, think about how you want your personal and professional life to look ten years from today. Be bold, creative, and genuine. Create clear goals that you find inspirational and worth working towards. At the end, you should have a picture of your life and career that is compelling enough to work through the barriers that will inevitably challenge you on the road to success. Feel free to add criteria and categories as you see fit.

MY GOALS

Income

Overall Finances

Achievements

Relationships

Contributions

Other

FAST TRACK CHALLENGE:

Take the top few highlights from your goals, write them on a separate piece of paper, and put it in your wallet or purse. Tape a copy on your computer screen or bathroom mirror. Carry your goals with you wherever you go. Reinforce in your mind the vision of what you are creating, and your mind will support and empower you in making that vision real.

CREATING A SHORT-TERM GOAL

You now have a vision for your life and career, and specific goals for the next ten years. The short-term future (now!) is when you start getting on track. Now is the time for making your longer-term goals and ambitions happen in the real world. By making significant progress in the next few days, weeks, and months, you can set yourself on a path that will have a profound impact on your life trajectory for the indefinite future.

In this section, think of one specific goal that can be accomplished in thirty days or less, and which will put you on target for achieving at least one of your ten-year career goals. It may be writing a new resume, getting a new job, applying to a degree program, enrolling in a certification course, negotiating a salary increase, or some other practical objective. The specific details don't matter, so long as you pick something that moves you in the right direction.

Your goal should be bold enough to inspire you and motivate action, and realistic enough that you genuinely believe it can be accomplished. A high level of belief is absolutely and completely necessary. Doubt and disbelief will prevent you from taking the right actions and maintaining the right attitude, which in turn makes success highly unlikely. Start with a goal you can believe in and expand as you build a track record of achievement.

As you engage in this process, remember that setting and managing goals will force you to develop new levels of strength and discipline, just like a new physical fitness program. If you have experience setting and achieving goals with consistency, step up the level of your game and go bigger. If your track record is less than spectacular, start with something a little smaller and start building a track record of success. The idea isn't to be perfect right away, but to get in the habit of consistently taking intelligent, purposeful action.

FAST TRACK CHALLENGE:

Define a practical goal that can be accomplished in thirty days or less. Write it here, and use the next section to create a plan for making it happen.

Short-term goal:

MANAGING YOUR GOALS THROUGH TO COMPLETION

It is a remarkable experience to set goals and allow the results to unfold without conscious effort. It just is. That said, you can't always afford to put your goals on a shelf and allow them to mature like fine wine. There are times in life when a more active and pragmatic approach is required. There are times when you HAVE TO succeed, like when you're out of work, restrictively underemployed, or stuck in a damaging career situation. In these circumstances, "someday" isn't good enough. You need results, and you need them *fast*. When you do, it's extremely useful to be able to set and achieve goals on a clearly defined timeline. Enter project management.

The following narrative, shared by a friend from Australia, will introduce several important themes for this section:

> *It was 2 a.m. on a Thursday when I had an insight that completely and totally changed my life. The project to which I'd dedicated two years of my professional life had just gone live, and all signs pointed to a massive success. Testing had gone well, off-shore support was on-line, and our local team was as prepared as possible for the expected uptick in transactions. This launch would mean millions in increased revenues for the company and huge*

accolades for me as the manager who pulled it all together. I logged off my computer, hit the lights, and headed out, happy and exhausted.

On the drive home I started thinking about what my team and I had accomplished. It was spectacular. The crowning achievement of my professional life, hands down, and I wanted to share it. I picked up the phone to call my husband, but realized he was undoubtedly asleep along with the rest of the civilized world.

As I thought about my husband it occurred to me that it had been months since I'd spent any quality time with my family. Literally months. All of my energy had gone into the project and everything else was on the backburner, including my health, friendships, and marriage. The result – my career was a success, but my personal life was a huge mess. Actually, it was worse than a mess…it was a complete disaster.

Inspired, I parked the car on the side of the highway, grabbed a pen and scrap of paper, and scribbled down half a dozen goals for myself and my family. I knew getting things turned around wouldn't be easy, but resolved myself to use every bit of skill and experience necessary to make them happen. Then I went inside and crashed for twelve full hours.

The next night I sat the family down at dinner and apologized for being a thoughtless jerk and asked forgiveness for letting things slide so badly. Then I shared the goals I'd created and asked them to join me as partners in making them happen. I'd love to say they were thrilled and everything went smoothly, but they weren't and it didn't. They were skeptical, to say the least. Fortunately, everyone was willing to be persuaded, and over the next few weeks we made some major shifts in our life together.

Over the next ninety days I lost over twenty pounds, enjoyed a weekly date night with my husband, and spent more quality time with my son and daughter than I had in years. I even made time to connect with old friends for a monthly ladies' night out. It was brilliant.

At the end of the process we sat down again and created our goals for the next three months, only this time my family was as engaged in the process as I was. At the very top of our list – a two week holiday on the coast with no laptops or work phones allowed.

Managing family goals has been every bit as challenging as my toughest work assignments, but the results have been even more rewarding. I've been managing projects for almost two decades, and can't believe I didn't think of this years ago.

Cheers,

Shelly T.
Australia

LEVERAGING THE TECHNIQUES OF PROJECT MANAGEMENT

"Far and away the best prize that life offers is the chance to work hard at work worth doing."

Theodore Roosevelt

❧

T he business world is a fantastic teacher when it comes to taking consistent, intelligent, and outcome-oriented action. In a free market economy, companies either figure out how to achieve their goals or they go under. The "produce results or die" reality has led to the development and evolution of project management as a formalized discipline. The most widely recognized leader in the field is the Project Management Institute (PMI), a not-for-profit organization with a presence in almost every major city in the world.

According to the Project Management Institute, a project is "a temporary endeavor undertaken to create a unique product, service, or result."[3] In other words, a project is something that happens within a specific time frame and is intended to produce a specific desired outcome. Simple.

The focus on delivering clearly defined results in a predefined time frame makes the practice of project management a great tool for those committed to achieving their most important goals. The next question is...

---

3   The PMI Project Management Body of Knowledge—PMBOK v1.3

HOW DO I BECOME A PROJECT MANAGER?

Viewed from a certain perspective, you already are. Nearly every facet of your life can easily be considered a separate and distinct project. Your career, your relationships, your health, your hobbies, even your vacations and intimate life could be broken into time blocks and categorized as "projects."

The bad news is no matter how miserably you might be failing at the job, you can't exactly replace yourself and hire a more competent resource. The good news is that you *can* upgrade your skills and dramatically improve your performance. The more proficient you become as a project manager, the more predictably and reliably you will be able to achieve your goals in ANY area of life. Leveraging project management as a personal skill makes sense, and more importantly, it makes a difference.

If you're already a project manager by profession, there are two ways you might want to approach this section. The first is to throw out everything you already know and take on the exercise as if you were learning the material for the very first time. A fresh approach and an open mind often lead to the discovery of new insights and experiences, so this path can be very effective and surprisingly rewarding.

The other option is to use this exercise as an opportunity to test your existing skills and expertise in a new context. You can take this process to a whole different level by incorporating the tools, technologies, and processes that make you successful in your professional life – things like project management software, action lists, task management tools, scheduling systems, and so on. Applying what you already know will deepen your skills, improve your odds of success, and bring a degree of comfort and familiarity to the process of setting and managing your personal goals.

Whether you're a rookie or an expert, use the next few sections as an opportunity to build the muscles required to manage your goals through to completion. You will begin the process by...

TRANSFORMING YOUR GOAL INTO A PROJECT

Experienced project managers will tell you that disciplined and intelligent action is only possible after defining a clear and achievable outcome. Until an outcome is defined, there is no possibility of project success. After all, how would you define success, and what would you be succeeding at?

A clear and measurable outcome is the essential first step in managing a project through to completion, and that's where the process of transforming your goal into a project will begin. Once your outcome is clearly defined, you will identify and clarify all of the intermediate steps and actions required for that outcome to happen in the real world. The last stage is where you do the actual work. The entire process of transforming your goal into a project can be broken into four basic steps:

Step #1: Identify the outcome

Step #2: Define the requirements

Step #3: Create an effective plan

Step #4: Manage the plan through to completion

A four-step process sounds like an oversimplification because *it is* an over-simplification. That said, each step hides many levels of complexity, and each of these four areas can be considered an area of expertise unto itself. In larger organizations, the separation of these steps into distinct job functions is often considered normal and necessary (if you have an interest in understanding the concepts and theory of project management, consider visiting the Project Management Institute website at www.pmi.org).

The process presented in this book is designed to make managing goals relatively simple, so the level of complexity has been minimized as much as possible without compromising effectiveness. It is also designed to be practical and experiential rather than theoretical. Instead of providing a great deal of detailed explanation, you will instead be walked through the process of creating and managing your project in the real world. In other words, don't just read this section, DO IT. The entire process is itself a Fast Track Challenge.

STEP #1: IDENTIFY THE OUTCOME

As Steven Covey might say, the first phase of project management is all about "starting with the end in mind." The emphasis is on defining your goal in a clear and concise way, and making sure there's a tangible result or product that can be measured to determine project success. That's stage one – defining what you're hoping to accomplish.

For this exercise, your goal (outcome) should be specific, measurable, and assigned a clear deadline. "Make more money" doesn't fit that criteria. How much more money? An extra dollar or an extra million? By when will you have more money? Similarly, "get a new job" is measurable, but not specific or time constrained. What kind of job? Waiter? Writer? Executive? What kind of company should it be? By when will you get the new job?

A goal that is conducive to project success might look like: "Write a world-class resume and have it posted on three major career sites by Friday at noon." The outcome is specific, the results are measurable, and the project has a clear deadline. On Friday at noon you will know whether or not you've done what you set out to do. Your resume will be complete and posted on three career sites, or it won't.

"Get hired as the sales manager for an Inc. 500 technology company and secure a 10 percent increase in salary by the end of January" is a more complex goal that fits the same criteria. By February 1st you'll either have a great new Inc. 500 sales management job and a 10 percent salary increase or not. You get the idea.

As a general rule, short projects are much more likely to succeed than longer ones, and simple projects are more likely to succeed than complex ones. Jim Johnson, project failure expert and founder of the Standish Group, says "Time is the enemy of all projects." Unless your business involves manufacturing fine clocks, he's right. In 2004 a study of over 23,000 projects was presented by the Standish Group at the PMI Global Congress. In that study it was demonstrated that a six-month software development project had almost a 55 percent chance at success, a twelve-month project dropped to about 25 percent, and a twenty-four-month project had less than a 10 percent chance of succeeding.[4]

That's a huge difference, and a big part of why so many projects fail. Long timelines and complex projects are a challenge even for seasoned experts, so keep your project short, focused, and simple. If your goal requires a significant investment of time and involves a high degree of complexity, it would be a good idea to start with something easy and build your way up to bigger challenges.

Either way, take a moment and rewrite or redefine your short-term goal. This goal will become the project you manage through to completion over the next few days or weeks.

Short-Term Career Goal (Project):

Deadline:

FAST TRACK CHALLENGE:

Having defined your goal, take a few moments to imagine yourself in the precise moment of getting it complete. Visualize yourself achieving success with as much color, sound, and clarity as possible. Picture yourself looking at the calendar and verifying that you did, in fact, finish on schedule (or perhaps a day early). Enjoy the sights and sounds around you, and let yourself feel proud of the accomplishment.

The more clearly you create this image in your mind the more likely you are to believe it will happen. The more you believe it will happen, the more

---

4   http://leadinganswers.typepad.com/leading_answers/files/large_project_risks.pdf

likely you are to take the actions required to make it happen. The more action you take, the greater your probability of success. Your vision becomes a self-fulfilling prophecy.

STEP #2: DEFINE THE REQUIREMENTS

A clear goal makes it possible to figure out what it will take to achieve project success. To effectively map out the steps, start by answering the question, "What resources, tools, and actions am I going to need during the course of this project?" Asking the question starts your mind working in the right direction, and answering it helps clarify what will need to get done.

In the last section we used "get hired as the sales manager for an Inc. 500 technology company and secure a 10 percent increase in salary by the end of January" as an example of a complex but well-defined goal. This is a challenging project that will allow us to cover the key elements required for using the project management process to succeed in simple and complex endeavors alike.

Achieving this goal would predictably require a resume, references, letters of recommendation, a list of target employers, an updated LinkedIn profile, and another dozen or so tools, actions, and resources. A first draft might look something like this:

My Project: Get hired as the sales manager for an Inc. 500 technology company and secure a 10 percent increase in salary

Deadline: The end of January

PROJECT REQUIREMENTS:
- An updated and highly effective professional resume
- Resume posted on CareerBuilder, Monster, and Dice.com
- Three or four letters of recommendation from past managers
- A target list of 20+ high tech companies within 25 miles of home

- A complete and updated LinkedIn profile
- Five recommendations on LinkedIn from past colleagues and managers
- An email to personal and professional friends about my job search
- Three or more expert recruiters engaged to work on my behalf
- Customized applications submitted to all 20+ target employers (directly or via referrals and recruiters)
- Interview with at least 4–6 companies in my target market
- Engage in salary negotiations with 2–3 prospective employers
- Secure two or more formal job offers
- Return a signed offer letter to my employer of choice

The requirements gathering process doesn't have to be long and complicated, and you don't have to get everything right the first time. Be as thorough as you can in a five-to-ten-minute brainstorm, and don't worry about being perfect or getting everything written in the right order. That comes later. For now, just think about all the things that need to happen between now and the end of your project, and write them down in a list format. More requirements and details will likely come up later, and you can always add them as appropriate.

FAST TRACK CHALLENGE:

Create your own requirements list with a rough outline of everything you'll need to do to complete your project and accomplish your goal.

STEP #3: CREATE A PLAN

With requirements defined, you can start building a viable project plan. The project planning process will include three basic elements: A Critical Path Analysis, an Action List, and a Timeline. The process doesn't have to be overburdened and complicated, but the more thorough you are, the more smoothly your project is likely to go.

The Critical Path comes first. The phrase sounds fancy, but creating a critical path is really just the process of organizing tasks into the right sequence. Some action items have to happen before others can be completed, others can be going on at roughly the same time, and some will have to wait until almost the end of the process. Pretty simple, really.

In our example it is clear that many other action items and requirements depend on "a highly effective professional resume." Until that first item gets handled you are unlikely to progress through to the stages of interviewing, reference checks, negotiation, and landing job offers. Due to the fact that many other actions depend on having this action handled, the requirement for a complete resume is a Level 1 item in the Critical Path Analysis.

At the same time, working on your resume doesn't preclude getting other things in motion as well. You can simultaneously secure letters of recommendation from past employers, verify your references, draft a list of target companies, and engage the help of your personal and professional networks. These items could also be listed as Level 1, as they support the actions that come later and aren't dependent on the completion of anything else. After applying the same logic to the rest of the requirements, our Critical Path Analysis might look something like this:

1.1 - CRITICAL PATH EXAMPLE

Critical Path – Level 1

1) Write a highly effective professional resume
2) Gather Letters of Recommendation
3) Verify contact details and validity of past references
4) Make a list of target employers in the local market

Critical Path - Level II

1) Post Resume to CareerBuilder, Monster, Dice

2) Update Profile on LinkedIn – use text from resume

3) Forward resume to local recruiters

4) Start submitting resume to list of target clients (two a day)

Critical Path - Level III

1) Interview with recruiters and prospective employers

2) Begin the salary negotiation process*

Critical Path - Level IV

1) Secure 2 or more written job offers

2) Select the best opportunity based on my personal and professional goals

3) Sign and return an accepted offer letter to my employer of choice

---

Once you have a critical path mapped out, you can peel back the layers on each individual requirement and identify the specific tasks and actions required to get it complete. A closer look at the requirement for "a highly effective professional resume" would reveal a handful of prerequisite actions that would help to fulfill the intention of that specific item.

For one, you might want to wait until you've read the section on Resume Writing to get a solid idea of what it takes to write a resume that stands out in a highly competitive market. From there, you could choose to mimic the resume format outlined in this book or go out to the Internet and search for a template that meets your personal goals and objectives (free templates are

---

*See part II for information on Win-Win negotiations

available at www.michaelbjunge.com, and a quick Google search will turn up hundreds of additional options).

After you have a good idea of how to put your resume together you can get down to the business of actually writing the content and putting it together into a cohesive document. In total, there are about four distinct action items built into the requirement for a highly effective professional resume.

1.2 – REQUIREMENTS EXAMPLE 1

> _**Requirement 1:**_ Write a Highly Effective resume
>
> Actions:
>
>   -Read Part II of _**Purple Squirrel**_
>
>   -Create or find an outstanding resume template
>
>   -Write the content for my resume
>
>   -Put the content together in a cohesive format

This process is repeated for each of the requirements on the critical path, and at the end there will usually be a couple pages worth of notes and action items. Looking at multiple pages of "to do" items can be a little overwhelming, but the next step, assigning a timeline, is extremely easy and allows you to spread the work out over a more manageable period of time.

1.3 REQUIREMENTS EXAMPLE 2

Requirement 1: Write a Highly Effective resume

Actions:	_Timeline_	_Duration_
-Read Resume Writing Section	Today (Now)	~40 min
-Create or find a resume template I like	Tomorrow	~20 min
-Write the content for my resume	Friday	~2 hours
-Put it all together in a cohesive document	Saturday	~1 hour

Requirement 2: Gather letters of recommendation

Actions:	_Timeline_	_Duration_
-Find copies of old letters of recommendation	Today	~15 min
-Send 3 recommendation requests on LinkedIn	Tomorrow	~10 min
-Call and email my past 2 bosses	Friday	~40 min
-Ask 2-3 past co-workers for letters (send email)	Saturday	~20 min

---

Here are a couple tips for setting a timeline and completing your goals on schedule:

- As you create your timeline, *be aggressive* and make a commitment to start NOW. Some people will encourage you to be realistic, but the longer it takes you to get in action, the more likely your project is to double or triple in length, or worse, fail altogether. Don't let that happen. Get started today and leave "realistic" to your competition; they can deal with realistic results while you're busy landing great jobs and climbing the corporate ladder.

- Frontloading the activities will help set the tone for the entire project. Prepare to do as much as possible today and tomorrow. An intense push at the beginning will allow you to complete all or many of the Level 1 and 2 items and set yourself up to stay on track with the rest of your timeline. Your project isn't a race, but kicking tail at the beginning will make it a lot easier to stay on track as the process moves forward.

- A good way to organize your Project Plan is to create a distinct page for each level of your Critical Path. Level 1 items will be on the first page, Level II on the second page, and so on until you've covered all of your project requirements. This will give a clear view of what needs to be done in approximately the order in which you'll be doing it. A page from your completed Project Plan might look something like this:

1.4 PROJECT PLAN EXAMPLE 1

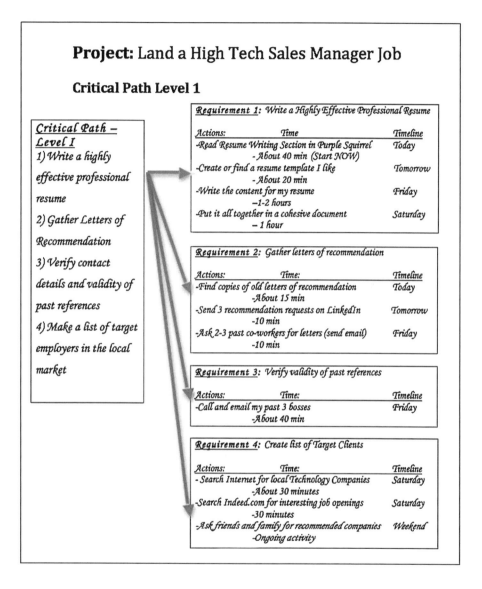

Project: Land a High Tech Sales Manager Job

Critical Path Level 1

Critical Path –
Level I
1) *Write a highly*
effective professional
resume
2) *Gather Letters of*
Recommendation
3) *Verify contact*
details and validity of
past references
4) *Make a list of target*
employers in the local
market

Requirement 1: Write a Highly Effective Professional Resume

Actions:	Time	Timeline
-Read Resume Writing Section in Purple Squirrel	Today
- About 40 min (Start NOW)		
-Create or find a resume template I like	Tomorrow
- About 20 min		
-Write the content for my resume	Friday
–1-2 hours		
-Put it all together in a cohesive document	Saturday
– 1 hour		

Requirement 2: Gather letters of recommendation

Actions:	Time:	Timeline
-Find copies of old letters of recommendation	Today
-About 15 min		
-Send 3 recommendation requests on LinkedIn	Tomorrow
-10 min		
-Ask 2-3 past co-workers for letters (send email)	Friday
-10 min		

Requirement 3: Verify validity of past references

Actions:	Time:	Timeline
-Call and email my past 3 bosses	Friday
-About 40 min		

Requirement 4: Create list of Target Clients

Actions:	Time:	Timeline
- Search Internet for local Technology Companies	Saturday
-About 30 minutes		
-Search Indeed.com for interesting job openings	Saturday
-30 minutes		
-Ask friends and family for recommended companies	Weekend
-Ongoing activity		

FAST TRACK CHALLENGE:

Create your project plan and assign a timeline to each of the action items and requirements in your Critical Path.

STEP #4: MANAGING YOUR GOAL (PROJECT) THROUGH TO COMPLETION

You have now transformed your goal into a project and created a viable plan for getting it done. What's left is to take consistent, intelligent, outcome-oriented action until the work is finished and you've achieved your goal. At this stage of the game there really aren't any secrets. What's required is simply to stay in action and make sure you're doing everything in your power to succeed.

Putting your timeline into a calendar system, creating daily action lists, and engaging an accountability partner are among the simplest ways to make sure you stay on track and achieve your goal. Scheduling specific blocks of time during which you'll get the work done can be a bit intrusive at first, but the "I'll get it done whenever I have time" approach doesn't usually work.

Without a system that supports staying within your timeline, the genuinely important actions will get pushed out in favor of shampooing the dog or watching reruns of *Seinfeld*. Scheduling specific blocks of time will help you avoid over cleaning your pets and under delivering on commitments.

As an added bonus, most computer based calendar systems come with wonderfully invasive pop-up alarms. If seeing the item on your calendar and action plan all day doesn't prompt you to take action, the little reminder alarm may just do the trick. Rather than dismissing, avoiding, or ignoring them, think of these reminders as an invaluable tool for empowering your own success.

In addition to setting up your project in a calendar, creating a daily action plan ("to do" list) is a very useful practice. While this step is almost completely redundant, for most people (myself included) it is also completely necessary. Some folks are predominately time oriented, others are more task oriented, and most are a combination of both. Creating a redundant system helps overcome the limitations associated with each style of self-management and provides a backup system in case one method fails. Redundancy may not be efficient, but it can be extremely effective.

FAST TRACK CHALLENGE:

1) Schedule 3-4 blocks of time into your calendar over the next two weeks, each at least two hours in length.

2) Create a series of "to do" lists that cover every action item in your project plan.

3. Put the "to do's" in your calendar and print redundant copies that can be kept near your desk or in a pocket.

FIND AND WORK WITH AN ACCOUNTABILITY PARTNER

Bob Bishop and I started working together at Romac International (now Kforce.com) in January 2000. Although Bob was an experienced salesman and I had just graduated college, both of us were rookies in the recruiting industry and were effectively starting from scratch.

In spite of great training and long hours, we found ourselves six months into the new job and struggling to produce serious results. Instead of going it alone, we decided to join forces and tackle the market together. Bob and I pushed each other day in and day out. When one of us would slack, the other would step in and apply pressure. When one of us needed help, the other was there to contribute. It worked both ways, and over the next twelve months we generated millions of dollars in revenues and propelled our office to the national leader board.

Our teamwork stood out so much that when several of the top performers in the company left to launch a new enterprise, Bob and I were invited to join them as part of the startup team. Our partnership continued, and as the company grew from $0 to over $50 million in annual sales we consistently outperformed every other team in the country (usually by a significant margin). While it's impossible to put a price tag on the value of a friendship, the hard numbers worked out to tens of millions in staffing revenues.

PICKING A PARTNER

There's no question that having outside support (and a little added pressure) can be a huge benefit to those wishing to accomplish something of value. Professional athletes and Olympians have coaches; people who succeed with diet and exercise programs usually have a trainer or buddy; and if you're going to achieve your goals, the odds of success go way up if you have a committed partner working with you.

To start, take a minute to identify two or three people with similar ambitions with whom you have a good solid relationship. Ideally, these will be people who are already in your life, who you respect, and whose goals are aligned with your own. The more closely your goals and ambitions are matched, the more valuable your partner will be to you, and vice versa. Write the names down here, along with why you think each person would be a good partner for you.

1)

2)

3)

Now pick up the phone and call the person on this list that you respect most (or better yet, meet them for lunch or a cup of coffee). When you connect, share what you are looking to accomplish and why you would like their help. Ask if he or she would be willing to help keep you on track for achieving your goals, and consider offering to do the same for them in return.

If they can't or won't, don't take it personally. Successful people are often busy and may already have a mentee or accountability partner in their life. If that happens, thank the person for their time and ask if you can still touch base from time to time. Then move on and connect with the next person on your list. In most cases, one of the people you identified will say yes. If not, you may have to extend your list to find a viable partner. That's okay. Keep moving forward.

Once you find someone to hold you accountable, share your plan with them. Literally. Hand them a written copy of the entire project plan you created. Ask their advice and opinion about the work you've done, what you could do to improve the plan, and what it will take to be successful. There's a good chance they'll see pitfalls, opportunities, and helpful actions that you've missed. Take their advice and put it to use as best you can.

If possible, schedule a daily or weekly call during which you're on the hook to provide updates on your progress and they have the opportunity to provide insight and guidance on what needs to happen next (and vice versa). Work together until your projects are complete and then start again with something new.

FAST TRACK CHALLENGE:

Put this book down and engage an accountability partner. Don't think about it. Pick up the phone and get it done.

TAKE ACTION, BE FLEXIBLE, AND ADJUST AS NEEDED

All the planning in the world is useless if you don't take action, so make a habit of doing as much as you can whenever you can. If you finish a project early, great! More power to you. Often, you will run into situations that slow you down or knock you off track. Life can be complicated, and you have to be ready to shift gears and change course when necessary. Getting off to a strong start can help smooth out some of the rough spots.

Even with a great start, a general guideline for project planning in the business world is to overestimate the time, energy, money, and effort required to complete a project by about two hundred percent (yes, double). Even with such a generous cushion built in, the typical project will "overrun" time and budget projections by a significant margin. People who fail to recognize that success is harder in reality than in theory set themselves up for the biggest failure of all—quitting. Don't fall into that trap.

One of the keys to good project management is being flexible enough to adapt to obstacles and circumstances and keep taking consistent action in the face of challenges. Instead of getting upset or frustrated when things don't go as planned, adjust your timeline, reset your expectations, and keep taking action. Expect challenges, and when you get stuck or need help, reach out to your accountability partner or a personal mentor.

Remember—even Bill Gates and Donald Trump have people they turn to for advice, and even they have to push and move project deadlines. Stay committed, make your goals a priority, and stay in action. This is being UNSTOPPABLE, and it is one of the most valuable skills you can develop as a professional (and as a human being).

KEEP GETTING BETTER

As you move forward, give yourself room to grow and improve. You aren't perfect now, you won't be perfect in a year, and you won't be perfect in this lifetime. Don't worry about being perfect and don't expect to be. Expect to get better. Expect to improve. Expect to learn and grow.

If you take consistent action you will continue to grow and improve indefinitely. Expect to get better at EVERYTHING you do right up until the day you die. Plan to be smarter, funnier, healthier, sharper, and more successful at age ninety than you are today. Then take consistent action to make it happen. After all, would you really want to experience the alternative?

PART II
Becoming an Opportunity Magnet

INTRODUCTION: A NEW PARADIGM

⚜

He was fifty-two years old and on the verge of a nervous breakdown when Charlie walked into my office. A year earlier his employer had outsourced their customer service department and call center operation off-shore to the Philippines. Without a team to manage, Charlie's job disappeared as well. The company offered a generous severance package, extended his health benefits for a year, and gently ushered him out the door. He felt bad for his team, but after three decades in the workforce, he was actually relieved to be out of a job. It was time for a break.

Fortunately for Charlie, he had plenty of liquid assets in his portfolio and more stocked away in savings and retirement funds, so the severance gave him a nice opportunity to wind down and figure out what he wanted to do with the rest of his life. He spent the next six months reading books, working around the house, and traveling with his wife. He was having such a good time that he decided to turn the unforeseen layoff into an early retirement. Their budget looked good, and though his wife worried, there was more than enough money to make it work.

Then, in late 2008, everything changed. Charlie went sailing with friends off the coast of Maine, and in the week between pulling anchor and putting back into port, his net worth dropped by over 20 percent. The stock market was in a free fall, and by the time all was said and done his severance package and insurance ran out and his total assets were down by more than half.

Almost overnight the prospect of retirement jumped fifteen years back into the future. Instead of scheduling his days around leisure, travel, and time with the grandkids, Charlie started worrying about paying bills in the short term. He even pondered the possibility of liquidating retirement assets.

After the raw shock began to wear off, he resigned himself to the fact that reentering the workforce would be a necessity for the foreseeable future. So much for fun. He quickly put together his resume, sent his interview suit out for dry cleaning, and called his old boss to make sure he'd get a good reference. Then he set about searching and applying for openings listed in the newspaper and online job boards.

Three months and over two hundred applications later, Charlie was still waiting for his first real interview. Sure, he'd gotten a couple of preliminary screening calls, but nothing that even remotely resembled a conversation with a qualified decision maker. Another three months slipped by and still nothing. Charlie started to panic.

By the time we shook hands he estimated that over four hundred hours had gone into his job search with no tangible results and no immediate prospects for turning things around. He was legitimately and understandably terrified. We talked for almost two hours, and before the end of the conversation Charlie had a plan for getting his job search on the right track.

Over the next two weeks he completely rewrote his resume, built a robust LinkedIn profile, stopped applying to long-shot jobs, and took advantage of a tool that helped him reach hundreds of prospective employers in a matter of minutes. After that he engaged a small army of recruiters who started proactively working on his behalf. In under a month he lined up a dozen interviews and had more calls coming in every day. Yes, there was work still to be done, but that was okay. Charlie had his mojo back, and it was just a matter of time before the right opportunity came knocking.

ATTRACTING MOTIVATED EMPLOYERS

"The question isn't who is going to let me; it's who is going to stop me."

Ayn Rand

❖ ❖ ❖

The biggest challenge in the modern job market isn't finding open job opportunities. There are tools available that make that incredibly easy. The problem now is differentiating yourself from the ever-increasing mass of competition. Online job postings often receive dozens or hundreds of applicant responses within the first few days, with total responses sometimes reaching into the thousands. Standing out against that degree of noise and distraction is a distinct challenge, one that requires the skillful use of strategy and tactics. That's one side of the equation.

The other side isn't about searching for jobs at all. It's about being searched for and sought after. Resume boards, social networking sites, search engines, recruiters, and keyword scanning software have combined to fundamentally change the employment game.

Now it's completely possible to get dozens of interviews and multiple job offers without ever sending an unsolicited job application. Every day more and more professionals are discovering that a few well-orchestrated shifts in their job search strategy can result in a landslide of interview activity. As you can probably imagine, it's a lot more fun being pursued than the other way around. Charlie certainly thought so.

The remainder of Part II focuses on techniques and concepts that will help you improve your effectiveness on both sides of the job search equation, pursuing and being pursued. As you work your way through the various chapters and sections, you'll notice that there's an intentional progression in the way the information is presented. You'll also notice that in addition to the Fast Track Challenges, there are lots of things you can DO. When a particular idea strikes you as useful, put the book down and try it immediately. Don't put it off until later, and don't wait for a Fast Track Challenge to spur you into action.

Your goal in this part of the book is to become an **Opportunity Magnet**, but getting to that level requires an investment of time and effort. Putting in the right amount of energy will empower you to attract the circumstances, situations, and people required to land your next job, and may ultimately lead to the career of your dreams. By the end of Part II you can expect to see a noticeable shift in your relationship to the job market and an equally important shift in the way the job market relates to you. This will start with a quick look at…

NEW TOOLS FOR THE EMERGING MARKET

Twenty years ago it could easily take weeks or months of digging through newspaper ads to identify a handful of quality job openings in a given industry and desired geographical area. Ten years ago it took days to sort through online and print ads, and even longer to submit applications. Today it can take minutes. Literally.

Regardless of your location and skill set, new tools have emerged that make it possible for employers to find you within a handful of keystrokes, or for you to find and apply for relevant opportunities anywhere in the world almost as easily. Several of the most valuable are highlighted in the following sections.

ONLINE RESUME BOARDS

Although they aren't exactly "new," online resume and job boards provide exceptional value to those positioning themselves to be pursued. From Monster and CareerBuilder to HotJobs, Dice, and hundreds of niche sites (including Craigslist), job boards provide the unique advantage of making your resume and information available to a highly relevant audience—the select group of people actively looking to hire new talent at the same time you're looking for work.

After typing in their key word criteria and hitting the "search" button, resume readers review the results of their query for high interest candidates. When they do, most will spend a few seconds scanning each resume to decide which prospects merit a closer look, rapid dismissal, or an immediate phone call. The key to getting maximum value from the job boards is a highly optimized resume, a topic that will be covered shortly.

PROFESSIONAL NETWORKING SITES

"The richest people in the world look for and build networks, everyone else looks for work."

Robert T. Kiyosaki

Professional networking sites are a direct extension of the broader category of "social networking" sites, with a specific focus on business activities rather than personal ones. The use of both types of networks will be discussed in greater detail in Part III, but for now the focus is on Internet based professional networking websites.

There are numerous players in this market at present, including Plaxo, Xing, and a few smaller niche sites, but only one clear leader: LinkedIn. LinkedIn currently holds the profiles of over one hundred million people, most of whom are middle and working class professionals. As a result, the site has become one of the most fertile grounds for recruiting and talent acquisition in the world, and is beginning to overtake many of the major job boards as a talent source for proactive headhunters and corporate employers.

Every day thousands of recruiters, HR professionals, and hiring managers sign in to LinkedIn and similar sites to identify and hire talent. They scan the sites for candidates using key word searches and other qualifying parameters such as location and employer name to find qualified individuals who fit their specific needs. Combined with the ability to network with candidates directly and request personal introductions, these sites provide rapid access to otherwise inaccessible resources.

As a job seeker, the biggest question with LinkedIn is how to use it to produce positive and predictable results. The answer is both simple and complex.

At a very basic level, you can attract attention and interest by building an online profile similar to the one you might create on any other job board. A completed LinkedIn profile will look and feel a great deal like a resume, and should be built following the same principles. There are other cool features you can include as well; a personal photograph, recommended reading lists, membership icons from various industry groups and associations, and more. All of these can help your target audience identify you as someone they may wish to hire and help you stand out from the competition.

2.1 – LINKEDIN PROFILE SCREEN SHOT[5]

Linked**in**® Go to LinkedIn Recruiter »

| Home | Profile | Contacts | Groups | Jobs | Inbox | Companies | News | More |

Become a Project Manager - Earn An MBA w/A Project Mgmt Specialization. No GMAT requir

Michael Junge
Leadership Recruiting/Sourcing at Google
San Francisco Bay Area | Information Technology and Services

Current	**Leadership Recruiting/Sourcing** at **Google**
Past	Recruiting Manager, National Development Director at Surrex Solutions Corporation
	Sr. IT Recruiter / Mentor / Consulting Services Manager at Surrex Solutions Corporation
	IT Recruiter at Kforce
Education	University of Arizona
	Universidad de Guadalajara
Recommendations	**22** people have recommended Michael
Connections	**500+** connections
Websites	Free Wheelchair Mission

The more complex and time-consuming methods for attracting attention are covered in Part III of this book. For now the bottom line is this: it's a very, very good idea to create a robust profile on LinkedIn and other similar sites, and to actively participate in online professional networking forums.

RESUME BLASTERS

The term "resume blasters" refers collectively to a group of online tools that send your resume out to a large, predefined audience. These tools fit somewhere in the middle of the pursuing/pursued equation, and as a general category of resource, they can be quite useful.

---

5   Author's Profile page on www.linkedin.com

The basic concept of a resume blaster is this: you sign up at a website that allows you to upload your resume and go through a checklist of skills, desired job types, geography parameters, and so on (create a profile). When you've completed the process, the tool sends an email to dozens, hundreds, or thousands of contacts who may be looking to hire for opportunities that fit your criteria. Presto-sendo and you're done. If you've drafted a great resume and introductory email, the calls might start coming within minutes.

Some resume blasters also offer a service that automates the process of posting your resume and profile on numerous job boards and niche sites. Not having to build individual profiles on every site can save dozens of hours of repetitive and mundane labor and that alone can be worth the price of admission.

The people on the receiving end of these resume blasts are typically recruiters (a.k.a. headhunters) and human resources professionals, though some direct hiring managers sign up for distributions from resume blasters as well. Rapidly getting in front of all three audiences is fantastic, especially because all three have similar goals and expectations.

Recruiters, for example, earn their living by placing candidates into job openings. Many are paid primarily or exclusively on commission, and that makes them a highly motivated ally in getting you hired. Similarly, a major part of the human resources function is talent attraction and retention. Like recruiters, HR professionals have a vested interest in finding the right people. If you can make them look good with management, they want you on board. Hiring managers are the ones whose necks are on the line for bottom-line business results, and if you can help them achieve their goals they want you on their team.

If you're qualified, capable, and bring a positive attitude to the table, all three audiences have a vested interest in getting you into a position where you can contribute. The more visible you are and the more people working on your behalf, the more likely it is that your dream job will come knocking (provided, of course, that you've put out the right information). A resume blaster can rapidly expand the number of these people and thereby accelerate the entire process.

JOB POSTING AGGREGATORS

Over the past decade the job board market has consolidated into a handful of major players (and countless niche sites), while search engines like Google and Bing have made the Internet much more closely connected. An offspring of the broader category of search engines, Job Posting Aggregators combine the purpose of the job boards with the single-source review capabilities of the search engines. As a result, they can be exceptionally useful when looking to track down your next position.

The aggregators are essentially search engines that crawl the Internet looking for job postings. They pull listings from the traditional online job boards like Monster.com, CareerBuilder, HotJobs, and Dice, as well as individual company websites, niche job boards, and the open web. The results are displayed, Google-style, in simple search engine interfaces that can be rapidly scanned for appropriate matches. Due to the fact that they search the majority of available sources simultaneously, these tools make identifying, evaluating, and applying for job opportunities exceedingly simple.

RECRUITERS

They aren't new either, but recruiters can be incredible career allies. As a client named Carl once said, "why should I spend hours reading and responding to job postings when I have a dozen recruiters out doing the hunting for me." Carl landed a Fortune 500 job and 30% pay increase without applying to a single listing. Perhaps he was onto something. Turning recruiters into "you" advocates is pretty simple. Be courteous, offer referrals, respond promptly, and operate with integrity. Easy.

2.2 INDEED.COM SCREEN SHOT 1[6]

indeed®
one search. all jobs.

what	where	
SQL Server DBA	Orange County, Ca	Find Jobs
job title, keywords or company name	city, state or zip code	Advanced Job Search

Post your resume - Let employers find you

My recent searches - clear

SQL Server DBA - Orange County, Ca

sql server dba - Menlo Park, CA

Employers - Find Resumes

2.3 INDEED.COM SCREEN SHOT 2[7]

indeed®
one search. all jobs.

what:	where:	
SQL Server DBA	Orange County, Ca	Find Jobs
job title, keywords or company	city, state, or zip	

SQL Server DBA jobs in Orange County, CA

My recent searches

sql server dba - Menlo Park, CA - 216 new jobs

» clear searches

Distance:
within 25 miles

▼ **Salary Estimate**
$60,000+ (60)
$80,000+ (35)
$100,000+ (14)
$120,000+ (8)
$180,000+ (1)

▸ **Title**

Jobs 1 to 10 of 68

Senior **DBA** - Oracle - DC106   Sponsored Jobs
Data Resource Management - Irvine, CA
software at the data layer in a **SQL server** environment using Transact-**SQL** Software
development skills in... net preferred **SQL Server** database administration...
Data Resource Management - 8 days ago

Sr **SQL DBA**
Partners Consulting Services - Laguna Hills - Foothill Ranch, CA
looking to hire a Sr **SQL DBA** for a Full Time position... experience as a Microsoft **SQL DBA**
required. Bachelors Degree Preferred IT Background Mastery of **SQL** basics...
Partners Consulting Services - 5 days ago

Sort by: **relevance** - date

Database Aministrator - **SQL Server**
Ingram Micro - Santa Ana, CA
Strong **SQL Server** Administration skills for **SQL** 2005... Minimum 2 years in Microsoft **SQL**
Server Database Administration with **SQL** 2005/2008 certifications...
Ingram Micro - 6 days ago - save job - block - email - more...

6   Screen shot of the www.indeed.com home page search screen, with search text entered by author.

7   Search results page from www.indeed.com with result from author's query

Although the market for Job Board Aggregators is young and likely to face changes over the next few years, two early leaders have emerged—Indeed. com and SimplyHired.com. Both are user friendly, highly accurate, and terrifically efficient. The companies that develop these sites use sophisticated algorithms, key word scanning technology, and text recognition software to pinpoint every posting in the public domain that fits the profile of a job opening. On average they do their job exceptionally well, and it is extremely rare to see anything other than a relevant job posting show up in the search results.

The long and short of it is that you can now search almost every public domain website simultaneously to identify job openings that match your search criteria, and you can do it in a matter of seconds. The most commonly reported inconvenience is that it can take a little longer to sort through the results and identify quality matches than it does on a single site (due to higher volume of total responses). It's also worth noting that many websites still require you to register before submitting a resume.

Inconveniences aside, the days of going from site to site and source to source to identify job openings are history. Your biggest problem going forward isn't finding open positions; it's figuring out which of them is actually worth submitting your resume to and distinguishing yourself from the competition. Not a bad set of problems once you know the insider tactics that will help your resume stand out and attract more viewers.

A FEW WORDS OF CAUTION

Before you jump ahead and start posting, blasting, and submitting your resume to the entire hiring world, take a deep breath and slow down. It's not time for that yet. First read the section on resume writing and invest the time required to construct a high impact profile before putting your information out to the market. Unless you do an outstanding job representing yourself, it's useless to get your resume out to a large audience. Actually it's worse than

useless. It's downright counterproductive. Wait until you have a fantastic resume and then consider using these tools. Not the other way around.

FAST TRACK CHALLENGE:

Practice exercising patience and wait until after reading the next few chapters to use the tools presented in this section.

THE MIND OF THE HIRING MANAGER

According to the clock in his car it's only 6:30 a.m., but John feels end-
of-day stress as he drives toward the office he's called home for the past twelve
years. He works for a solid organization and is grateful for his job, but the past
two years have been rough. Accounting software sales are down across the
industry and his company has been hit especially hard. Downsizing whittled
John's team of thirteen down to eight, and the rest of the company is in exactly
the same boat.

In spite of sagging revenues and horrific morale, the executive team recently
called the staff together to deliver an optimistic ninety-day forecast. The financial resources for the company had been stabilized, so the layoffs were finished
and there would be no further pay cuts in the immediate future. Excellent
news. The balance sheet showed a profit for the first time all year, and to top
things off, the sales team reported an extremely healthy pipeline of qualified
prospects, many of whom were lined up and ready to buy.

Things were looking up, the CEO said, and provided the next release of
their flagship product shipped on schedule and met customer expectations, the
company would turn a profit this year.

It all sounds like great news to most of the company, but John has
a different take on their situation. As manager of the team in charge of
developing the product, his take is that they are in serious, serious trouble.
The layoffs were bad, but things got a lot worse when his best programmer
gave notice last Friday. The loss of a key team member left him with four

months and a team of seven to complete a twelve-person job and keep the company from going under. Coaching Little League would have to wait another year.

John's stomach twists in knots as he pulls into the company parking lot. He has no idea how he's going to pull off the miracle required of him, but he does know one thing. He knows he's going to need an expert programmer on his team fast. Fast like yesterday.

After a quick talk with Human Resources and the company VP, the budget for a replacement hire is approved and a position description is drawn up. By 9 a.m. the HR manager has posted the new job description on two major job boards and set the systems up to route resume responses directly to John. Not feeling particularly optimistic, John starts his morning meeting with the development team by asking if anyone knows an accounting systems programmer who might be interested in a new job. No one does.

Two meetings and four hours later John grabs his lunch out of the fridge and logs onto the email system. His Inbox shows 117 new messages, more than triple what he'd have normally expected. A virus, he thinks. You've got to be kidding me.

John clicks open the Inbox and starts to scan the subject lines, wondering exactly what variety of horror the rest of the day holds in store for him. His jaw drops. It's not a virus. Far from it. More than eighty of the messages are responses to the job posting. As he stares at the screen two more responses pop in. He smiles for the first time all morning. Wow, he thinks, this is going to be easier than expected.

Two hours and eighty-seven emails later John walks away from his desk in complete and utter disgust. Of the entire list of respondents, only four look even remotely qualified. Two of them are located in India and would require a lengthy visa sponsorship process before working in the U.S. No dice. The other two are high-end consultants from the East Coast and way out of his budget. The majority of the resumes are from truck drivers, accountants, recent college grads, and off-shore development companies. Good people, no doubt, but not what he needs right now. A sinking despair sets in as John grabs his laptop and walks into his next meeting. He succeeds in avoiding email for the rest of the day but still doesn't get home until almost 8 p.m.

By morning the stack of messages has grown back to over a hundred, most of them resume submittals. Unwilling to spend hours reading junk responses again, John quickly scans the list to see just how hopeless the situation might be. His eyes are drawn almost immediately to an email halfway down the list with a subject line that reads "Expert Software Developer with 10+ Years of Accounting Systems Experience." He perks up a little, feeling a resurgence of hope.

John clicks open the email and sees a bulleted list of accomplishments and a pleasant introductory note from the applicant, a local woman named Mary. As he reads more closely he notices that she's listed a number of well-respected companies as past employers, including one prominent competitor. She's also included a link to her personal website, which shows screenshots and images from some of the applications she has helped develop in the past. John quickly reviews her resume, confirms that her background is on target, and picks up the phone to schedule an interview.

THE JOB OF THE JOB SEEKER

As a job seeker, your job is to make it easy for employers to recognize your ability to help THEM. It's that simple. When you submit your information to an employer, the highest probability is the person on the other side of your resume is like John; overworked, understaffed, and highly stressed. The character in this illustration is fictional, but the experience is one shared by employers around the world. Managers are looking for people who can help them achieve specific goals and objectives – people who will make their lives just a little less stressful and chaotic.

Recruiters and HR professionals serve as intermediaries that help streamline the process and minimize the stress that hiring puts on managers who already have more than enough on their plates. Being effective intermediaries requires that these people become proficient in sorting through massive amounts of information and making instantaneous decisions about where to invest their time and energy.

As they search for qualified talent, all three audiences engage in a process that involves ELIMINATING possible candidates at least as much as identifying them. Most read the resume, subject line, email, and other correspondence with the express intention of disqualifying applicants that don't fit the bill. Doing so frees them up to focus their time and attention on the small handful of individuals who are readily identified as high-quality matches.

Eliminating candidates this early in the process isn't evil or unfair – it's a matter of survival. When there are hundreds or thousands of resumes to sort through (or more), it is literally impossible to read every single one in detail. There simply aren't enough hours in the day. As a result, the pros learn to rely on shortcuts.

As a job seeker you can be a victim of this reality, or you can use it to your advantage. Using it to your advantage means writing your resume and related communication in a way that works with these shortcuts and helps the other party quickly recognize your ability to add value. That's where the fundamentals come in.

MASTERING THE FUNDAMENTALS

"First master the fundamentals."

Larry Bird

☯

eadhunters are paid specifically and exclusively for their ability to identify talent and get people hired. The best of the best earn nearly as much as the average professional athlete or corporate CEO. To effectively compete in an industry where top performers routinely earn hundreds of thousands of dollars per year, serious headhunters rely on closely guarded strategies for getting their applicants noticed and securing preferential treatment in the hiring process.

The next few sections of this book are dedicated to exposing a handful of the insider strategies that are passed down and shared amongst top performers in the staffing industry. These tactics allow a recruiter to attract attention to a given resource, bypass the screening out mechanisms used by resume readers to eliminate applicants, and guide their candidates through to a successful hire.

Applying these techniques as a job seeker will help you accomplish the same goals – to instantly grab the attention of your target audience, avoid the rapid elimination mechanism, and gain a significant edge throughout the hiring process. These tactics are among the fundamentals that will help you transform yourself into an Opportunity Magnet.

WRITING A HIGH-IMPACT RESUME

Among the resources available for helping attract the attention of relevant employers, the resume stands alone in one distinct way—it offers the chance to leverage One Way Communication. One Way Communication is exactly what the phrase implies – an opportunity to present information, sway opinions, and create a desired response without any discussion or debate. Given that you have a very narrow window in which to deliver your message, and given that the ability to do so can dramatically affect your entire career, it makes sense to capitalize on this opportunity to the absolute best of your ability.

Over the course of this section you will learn rules and strategies for using your resume to produce maximum value and effect. Before getting into the specifics of how to construct a resume—what to write, what not to write, how to write it, and so on—let's take a moment and challenge your thoughts and assumptions about something you probably take for granted…the resume itself.

What, exactly, is a resume?

Rather than jump to conclusions or fall back on preconceived notions or opinions, think about that question for a minute. What is a resume? Write down the first thoughts that come to mind:

A resume is…

If you're like most people who answer this question, you probably came up with a phrase or sentence to the effect of "a resume is an overview and summary of personal skills, interests, employment history, attributes, and professional experience."

Sound about right? Now think about this: did your response relate in any way to the PURPOSE or function of a resume? Did it speak to what your resume is designed to do? For that matter, what is the purpose of a resume? What is it supposed to do? Take a minute and complete the following sentence:

The purpose of a resume is_____.

If you really thought this out, you're probably much closer to understanding the goals of this section than you were just a few minutes ago. What your resume "is" is far less important than what your resume is designed to DO. If you answered these questions honestly and thoroughly, you've recognized a few basic responses - "to help me land a new job" or "to help me market myself to prospective employers" or "to help me get interviews" – all encompassed by the underlying theme of generating a specific desired response from a well-defined target audience.

Your resume, like everything else, is designed to serve a purpose. A very specific purpose. To be very direct, specific, and blunt ...

Your Resume is a Sales Letter

Yes, you read correctly. Your resume is a sales letter. The idea of marketing or selling yourself may be a bit uncomfortable, and while that's understandable, it is also a bit naive. Opinions and judgments aside, you are absolutely using your resume to market, sell, and promote yourself to prospective employers. It's not a question. It's a fact.

If it makes you feel better you can think of it as "licensing" rather than selling or marketing, but you'd be better served by just grasping the basic concept and learning how to use it to your advantage. Marketing yourself is simply a way to ensure that the value you can add to a company is obvious and clearly defined for your target audience. Doing so encourages prospective employers to interview and hire you, and ultimately requires that they provide adequate compensation for your time and talent.

At the end of the day, your resume is a sales letter written to market your skills and experiences to prospective employers. That's it. It's that simple, and once you understand that concept, it's going to change the way you think about resume writing and job applications for the remainder of your career.

The next question is: How do I use this knowledge to write a more effective resume? We'll get to that in just a minute. First, take a moment to reflect on...

THE GUIDING PRINCIPLE OF RESUME WRITING

"Integrity is the essence of everything successful."

Buckminster Fuller

Having learned (or been reminded) that a resume is actually a marketing tool, it's time to bring up a point on ethics. You can think of it as the Guiding Principle of Resume Writing (because that sounds fancy), but it's really just common sense and old fashioned honesty.

<u>Guiding Principle</u>: ALL information you present on your resume and throughout the submittal process must be truthful, factual, and accurate. Always.

This may sound obvious, but years of interviewing have demonstrated that when it comes to the resumes people write, nothing should be taken for granted. The simple fact is that many, many people take significant liberties when writing their resumes and going through the interview process. It happens, and often goes unnoticed until it really counts (like when an interviewer asks probing questions, or a potential employer conducts a detailed background check).

Practically speaking, resume "fudging" can lead to serious consequences, including but not limited to career setbacks and unpleasant legal action. You've probably seen news stories about executives busted for misrepresenting their skills and experiences and major government players ousted for resume misstatements. The same happens in a much quieter way to those in lower-level positions who mislead employers through blatant misstatements and inaccurate resume claims.

Lies and misrepresentations catch up with all of us in the end – even when no one else discovers them. In order to succeed at an extraordinary level, integrity must be at the core of your identity. Integrity ensures that your worth is intrinsic and not subject to the ups and downs of the job market or your employment status. Constructing your resume with integrity creates a platform of integrity for your entire career. Failing to do so is like building a boat out of sugar cubes; it may float for a while, but eventually it's going to sink.

The remainder of the material on resume writing is designed to make sure you're able to write a competition crushing resume with ethics and integrity. Doing things right doesn't have to be a disadvantage. To the contrary, when combined with the other tactics covered in this book, doing things right will provide a distinct edge over your less informed counterparts. Going forward, you aren't going to have to take liberties. You'll get noticed, interviewed, and hired without having to play games or compromise your integrity.

THE NEW RULES OF RESUME WRITING

Given that your resume is a sales tool, and given that you're going to be presenting all included information accurately and truthfully, there are many clever ways to polish and refine a resume that fall well within the bounds of good ethics and high integrity. With the rapidly accelerating pace of decision-making, effective positioning of facts and details is an absolute necessity. Over the next few sections you're going to learn how to creatively present your skills and experiences in a way that works with the resume reading tricks and short-cuts used by the three primary hiring audiences.

For starters, it's important to remember that your resume has a window of roughly five to ten seconds to catch the attention of anyone reading it. You have to be prepared to make a very fast and positive first impression in order to move things to the next level. For that to happen, your resume needs to be optimized for maximum results. This fact is the driving force behind the New Rules of Resume Writing. These are:

Rule #1: Know Your Audience
Rule #2: Get to the Point
Rule #3: Use Hybrid Titles
Rule #4: Your Resume Is Alive

RULE #1 – KNOW YOUR AUDIENCE

You're already familiar with the plight of hiring managers. They're over-worked, understaffed, and running on limited time. The other two audiences, recruiters and HR professionals, have equally challenging circumstances. They're tasked with sorting through millions of online profiles and dozens or hundreds of job applications and zooming in on the much smaller number of individuals who are qualified and capable of succeeding in a given job.

The long and short of it is that everyone in your target audience is depending on shortcuts to help make rapid and intelligent decisions about where to invest their time and energy. Key word scanning, resume skimming, and title surfing (just reading job titles) are among the most common tactics for shortening the amount of time dedicated to reviewing each individual resume.

All of the major job boards and professional networking sites enable these shortcuts through the use of simple algorithms that determine which results will be displayed first. This is typically based on key word relevancy, key word density, title, and posting date. The more matching key words you have in your resume and the more frequently they are used, the closer to the top of list you will appear (especially if your profile is updated on a regular basis).

Your audience has limited time and lots of profiles to review, and it's a very good idea to use this knowledge to your advantage. If you want to write a great resume, start by reading as many job descriptions as you can. As you do, pay particular attention to the words, phrases, and titles used by the people who are searching for individuals with your skills and experience. Understanding what your audience is looking for and using the right language on your resume will help you attract more viewers, more interest, and more interview activity.

RULE #2 – GET TO THE POINT

You've heard the saying "you never get a second chance to make a first im-pression." It's as true in resume writing as it is in dating. One glance often sets the tone for an entire first date, and that same infinitesimally small opening is what you can reasonably expect from a resume reader. That means you have to get right to the point and show them exactly what they're looking for, and do so without a lot of preamble and wasted space.

One of the first secrets shared with me by staffing industry legend Mike Ellis was to treat the first page of a resume like valuable real estate. Like the front page of a newspaper, it should be used to rapidly deliver a highly relevant and targeted message to attract the attention of a specific audience. The lesson is even more relevant today than it was years ago.

The key word scanning software used by the vast majority of job boards and professional networking sites automatically highlights the words and phrases targeted in a given query. As a result, resume readers can instantly see whether or not a given profile is rich in skills relevant to the position they are looking to fill. That's one of the reasons experienced professionals can get away with a scan of a few seconds before deciding whether to pick up the phone or move on to the next candidate.

As a result of the quick scan methodology, the majority of your focus will go into the construction of the first page of your resume, which should be fine-tuned until every aspect is optimized for maximum results. At a very basic level, this means moving the most relevant information and details right up to the front – the front of your resume and the front of each section that comprises your resume.

This especially relates to the key words and phrases that are actively being sought out by your target audience. When a hiring manager, recruiter, or human resources professional conducts their five or ten second scan of your resume, their browser should highlight numerous words and phrases that instantly let them know exactly what makes you qualified for the job at hand.

Front-loading the pertinent content allows a quick scan of your resume to return a wealth of relevant information, and that's what it takes to capture the attention of the hiring audience. This positive first impression buys you the time you need to make a compelling case to take things to the next level, and that's the real goal of resume writing: to move forward into the interview process with highly motivated employers.

RULE #3: USE HYBRID TITLES

In addition to key word scanning, one of the most common ways that resume readers eliminate candidates is by title surfing, or quickly scanning the titles used in a given resume or candidate profile. Unrelated or confusing titles offer a quick excuse for saying no and moving on to the next prospect, saving time and eliminating unproductive conversations.

This helpful shortcut has one glaring problem: lots of companies use naming conventions that are unique and seemingly unrelated to those of others in their industry. That means the titles used in one organization may not translate to the titles used in another. As a result, high-quality candidates are often missed or overlooked by well-meaning resume readers simply because their employer used the wrong words to describe their job function.

To combat the inherent limitations of the title surfing approach, many staffing experts recommend the use of "functional" titles. What that means is employing the use of titles on your resume that mimic or mirror the naming conventions used by a particular industry or specific employer. Provided the new title accurately reflects the nature of the work you did, this is considered a legitimate practice and can provide a definite competitive advantage.

In theory, there shouldn't be any issues with following the functional title approach. In practice, however, it sometimes leads to questions and complications during the reference checking and employment verification process. When the title on your resume doesn't match the one stored in the HR database of your past employer, a red flag may go up. Even though many employers understand the adjusting of titles for functional reasons, some aren't.

An equally effective and much safer practice is to use "hybrid" titles. A hybrid title allows you to take advantage of the same principle as a functional title, but with a much lower risk of unintended negative consequences. Instead of completely changing your given title and adopting one that speaks more directly to your target audience, a hybrid title allows you to do both at the same time.

Imagine, for example, that your current title is Network Administrator and your job requires you to provide engineering level support for a Windows server and Cisco router environment. You are applying for an opportunity where the title is Systems Engineer, and the job duties are Windows Server administration and Cisco engineering. An appropriate title for your resume might be Network Administrator (Windows and Cisco Systems Engineering). You can write it a number of ways, but the most common are to use a comma, set of parentheses (preferred), or a forward slash. For example:

Network Administrator / Windows and Cisco Systems Engineer

Network Administrator, Windows and Cisco Engineer

Network Administrator (Windows/Cisco Engineering)

The title accurately reflects your skills and title, as well as the specific key words your audience is looking to find. That means you've got a great chance of catching the eye of the resume reader and are unlikely to raise any red flags during the employment verification process. That's a clear win-win.

When posting your resume on job boards and networking sites it's not possible to be quite as precise as when submitting to a specific position, but you can take advantage of the hybrid title principle all the same. Instead of attempting to match your title and key words to a particular job opening, you can include your current title followed by a small cross section of the words and phrases most commonly used by employers searching for a candidate with your skill set (no more than a few words at most). If you've done your homework, this should be a relatively easy task.

RULE #4: YOUR RESUME IS ALIVE

Because the level of competition keeps increasing and the window of opportunity for making a positive impression keeps getting smaller, the old idea of a single version resume is dead. In order to effectively differentiate yourself, your resume must be more than a "static" informational page. It has to be able to change and adapt in order to fulfill its purpose, especially when you are on the side of pursuing employment.

Obviously you can't write a brand-new resume every time you apply for a job. That'd be crazy. What you can do is create a standardized resume for each *category* of position you're actively going to pursue. These "master" resumes will highlight the specific skills and experience that make you uniquely qualified for a given type of opportunity, with the information organized and sequenced appropriately for your target audience in that niche space.

Master resumes can be quickly customized and revised to effectively present the most relevant skills and experience for specific opportunities while in pursuit mode, and help you rapidly stand out when positioning yourself to be pursued.

MINDSET AND MECHANICS

Now that you know what your resume is (a sales letter) and are familiar with the Guiding Principle and New Rules, it is nearly time to get down to the actual *writing* portion of resume writing – the "mechanics" if you will. Before you do, there's one final piece of preparatory work, and that's adopting the proper mindset to write an effective resume.

MINDSET

One of the biggest mistakes Charlie made during his first four hundred hours of job search was settling for a horribly mediocre resume. In spite of a background filled with highly relevant skills and experiences, his resume was less than a page in length and carried almost no content any employer would find meaningful. There was no mention of the tools and technologies he had used, no reference to the quantifiable results he'd produced, and nothing designed to let an employer know the value he could bring to their organization.

Like many people, Charlie felt uncomfortable writing about himself in a positive way. Rather than seeing his resume as a useful marketing tool and investing the time required to make it extraordinary, he considered it a necessary evil and tried to get it done as fast as possible. He thought that if he banged out a quick resume he'd be able to move more quickly into the rest of the hiring process. As a result, he got stuck sending out hundreds of copies of his resume without ever moving into the interview phase. Not good.

Like all sales and marketing pieces, there are more and less effective ways of producing a positive response with a resume. In the Direct Mail Industry a typical marketing piece produces a "buying" response about 1 percent of the time. Ineffective campaigns may receive only a handful of customer inquiries per thousand pieces mailed or no response at all.

The same is true in resume writing, except that a well-written resume will elicit a response far more often than even the best direct marketing piece. A poorly constructed resume, like a badly designed mailer, may not produce any positive responses at all. Imagine how many hours you might have to spend looking at job postings in order to secure even a half-dozen interviews at a response rate of even five or ten percent. Painful, right?

Unless you want to fall in line with normal, you have to do a better-than-average job putting together your resume. The resume is about you, so your first inclination will be to think about and describe your skills and experiences in the ways that sound best to you. Unfortunately, that's exactly the wrong approach. Your resume isn't about you. Not really. It's about the person you're writing to and how you can make their life easier.

Great marketers know that the best way to sell a product isn't to focus on the product at all – it's to focus on how the product solves a problem that is already bothering their potential customer. In the context of a company looking for talent, the problem is inadequate resources, a growth opportunity, the risk of losing revenue, or something similar. Your resume should help a potential client recognize that you are a solution to one of their problems, a pathway to capitalizing on one of their opportunities, or both. The right mindset for resume writing is *customer-centric*.

RESUME MECHANICS

Once Charlie understood that his resume was a marketing piece, his next question was "Okay, so what exactly does that mean? How do I put it together the right way?" It was a great question. What he needed was a proven framework around which he could organize relevant content and useful information. For professionals, that's where the mechanics begin – with the adoption of an effective and proven framework.

In this context, a framework can be defined as a consistent organizing structure that dictates where and how information will be displayed. Since the resume is a sales and marketing piece, the framework selected must make it easy for a prospective customer (employer) to find the key pieces of information that let them know it's a good idea to move forward in the "buying" process.

Their ultimate goal may be solving a problem or seizing an opportunity (or in the case of a recruiter, earning a commission), but most resume readers think of these items in terms of specific skills, key words, quantifiable results, educational background, certifications, attributes, and experiences. They will be looking for clues that let them know you are, in fact, a solution to their problem or a pathway to their opportunity.

Adopting a simple, logical, and proven framework will allow you to showcase your most relevant skills and experiences clearly, effectively, and in a way that speaks directly to the needs of the customer. Doing so empowers you to focus on delivering high-impact information quickly and with high frequency, and it all starts with the creation of page one.

LOCATION, LOCATION, LOCATION

The front page of your resume is by far the most important. It's what read-ers will see first, and in many cases is the only part of your resume they will review before picking up the phone to schedule an interview. If the first page of a resume is valuable real estate, everything a reader sees immediately upon opening it is like beachfront property in Newport Beach.

The message delivered in the first few sections of your resume will almost certainly determine whether or not the rest of it gets looked at all. Most re-sumes don't. In order to maximize the immediate impact your resume has on the hiring audience, the framework for the first page should include as many of the following key elements as possible:

An Education Section, but ONLY if you have a completed college or post-graduate degree, ideally in a directly related field. Degree programs that haven't been completed automatically go to the bottom of the re-sume (or get deleted altogether), making room for more impactful and relevant information. **Certifications and Training Sections,** but only if the information included is relevant to your specific audience or dem-onstrates a competency they are likely to perceive as valuable. Unrelated certifications and training go at the bottom of the resume or disappear completely.

A Skills Summary that covers all tools, technologies, and skills relevant to your audience. It can and *should* be loaded with keywords and phrases, but only those that can be backed up in conversation. This section is designed to be an attention magnet, not a deal-killer. You want to draw the focus of a resume reader without setting yourself up to bomb the interview.

A Professional Summary of at least a few highly relevant bullet points. These bullet points will highlight the skills, key words, and accomplish-ments that most directly relate to the type of opportunity being pursued. This section is the centerpiece of the first page and should be engineered with great care and attention.

Work Experience that reinforce and showcase the key words and skills referenced in the earlier sections. To the best of your ability, include the complete description of the experience gained at your most recent employer. If it doesn't all fit, include the employer name, a hybrid title, and at least a few lines of content describing your relevant on-the-job experience. If needed, the rest can spill over onto page two.

EDUCATION, CERTIFICATIONS, AND TRAINING

These categories are related and will take only a small amount of resume space, so they have been lumped together for a brief summary-style review. An Education section is usually dedicated to four-year and post-graduate degree programs, but may also include relevant junior college and two-year degrees.

> Interviewers often ask questions based on the information presented on your resume, so don't write anything you're not prepared to back up in conversation *and* on the job.

Training typically refers to vocational programs, industry specific trainings, "in house" programs offered by past employers, certification courses, and any other professional training that may be applicable.

Certifications are, well, certifications. They demonstrate knowledge and expertise in a specific skill set, technology, or domain, and when relevant, can be a critical differentiator between candidates.

A completed *and* relevant four-year or post-graduate degree will ALWAYS show up at the very top of your resume because degrees are a critical screening factor for many top employers. A relevant degree establishes credibility and makes a positive first impression that can provide a huge leg up on the competition. That's why it goes first. If you have a college-level degree in a related field, showcase it. If your degree is complete but in an unrelated field, it can stay at the top or be moved to the bottom of the resume at your discretion (though it is worth noting that a completed degree is almost always perceived as a positive).

Similarly, industry or skill related certifications and training programs can have a markedly positive impact on a resume reader. It's a great idea for an accountant to show off their CPA, a project manager to highlight their PMP certification, and for you to showcase any certifications and training programs that establish you as a competent, qualified expert in your field. These will go right at the top of your resume, just below the Education section.

In general, you will want to include the name of the institution where your education or training took place, the specific title of the program you completed, the specific rank, certification or degree you earned, and the year in which it was completed. You will take up as little space as possible with this information, one to two lines maximum per degree, training program, or certification. Condensing this information will help make sure you get as much mileage out of this space as possible. For example:

Education

Bachelor of Management Information Systems, University of Arizona – 1999

MBA in Finance, UC Irvine – 2004

Certifications

Project Management Professional (PMP), PMI – 2006

Training

The Theory of Constraints / Jonah Training, The Goldratt Institute – 1998

Project Management Curriculum, Surrex Project Solutions – 2003

In a very short amount of space you can express a great deal of highly relevant and impactful information. The main caveat here is to be appropriate to your target audience. If you are looking for a job as an accountant, your mixologist training and bartender certification probably won't be all that meaningful. The top of your resume should only be used for information that will HELP you. Everything else can move to the bottom or disappear completely.

FAST TRACK CHALLENGE:

Create your own Education, Certifications, and Training Sections (as relevant) using the following format and making adjustments as appropriate:

Education
Degree, Institution (GPA if outstanding) – Year
Degree, Institution (GPA if outstanding) – Year

Certifications
Certification Title, Certifying Body – Year

Training
Training Name, Training Entity – Year
Training Name, Training Entity – Year

THE SKILLS SUMMARY

A Skills Summary (aka Key Words section) provides a front page space for showcasing and frontloading the relevant words and phrases sought by resume readers as they scan for viable candidates. It should include as many key words and relevant phrases as possible and be organized as logically and intuitively as possible.

Consider the sample Skills Summary of a hypothetical candidate presented below. This "person" has a background in database and software engineering with an emphasis on Microsoft SQL Server. As you look at this example, pay attention to the format and structure as well as the specific content and key words.

Although your information will probably be very different, you'll want to create a similar structure as you build and customize your own Skills Summary. It's also okay to create a completely different look and feel to your Skills Summary, as long as it meets the objective of providing the right key words to your target audience in an organized and logical way. For example:

RDBMS: MS SQL Server v 2008/2005/2000, Oracle 8i/9i/10g, MS Access.

Database Tools: SQL 2005/2008 SSIS and SSAS, SQL EM, SQL Profiler, SQL Query Analyzer, Index Analyzer, DTS tools, SQL Agents, SQL Alerts, SQL Jobs, SQL Mail.

Tools: SQL Scribe, Visio.

Front End Tools: Developer/2000, Visual Basic v4.0/5.0/6.0, C#, MS Access, Visual Source Safe.

Software: DB2, CICS, JCL, VSAM, IIS.

Languages: Java 1.2/2.0/2.1, COBOL, Perl, C# (.Net v2.0, 3.0, 3.5), VB6, JIL, T-SQL.

Other: Database Design, Database Engineering, Data Migration, ETL, Project Management, SDLC Methodologies (Waterfall, Agile, Scrum), UML, Visio, MS Project, Office.

There are a few important details to notice in this summary. For one, the information is organized logically and efficiently, allowing for easy review and rapid key word scanning. For another, the database related skills show up at the top of the summary and toward the beginning of each section. This provides added emphasis and lets the audience know that the candidate considers these skills to be among their most valued assets.

Last, a number of the specific skills include a version number (e.g. - SQL Server 2008/2005/2000). A version number may seem like an insignificant detail, but in reality it can be a crucial differentiator between candidates with similar skill sets. Having the exact version of a given tool or technology minimizes the startup and training time required to become productive, and that's always perceived as valuable to an employer.

Using a clear organizational structure, front-loading key word content, and including specific version numbers can help make your resume "magnetic" and engaging to a very specific target audience. When someone goes looking for a candidate with a specific background or toolset and finds you, the odds of receiving a quick call or email to schedule an interview are quite high.

Every industry has unique classification systems, so there aren't generic or universal categories for organizing the information in this section. Even so, the basic format and structure presented below is highly effective and can be shared across almost all industries and professions. Your personal skills summary will be customized and tailored to fit your specific market and audience, and you can find additional examples for a variety of professions at www.michaelbjunge.com.

FAST TRACK CHALLENGE:

Create your own Skills Summary using the following format and inserting the categories, key words, phrases, and version numbers appropriate to your background and industry. Don't worry about mimicking the format exactly, but do make sure to keep the information organized logically, efficiently, and with the relevant material up front:

Category: Skill v1/2/3, Skill v1/2/3, Skill, Key Word, Key Phrase

Category: Skill v1/2/3, Skill v1/2/3, Skill, Key Word, Key Phrase

Category: Skill v1/2/3, Skill v1/2/3, Skill, Key Word, Key Phrase

Category: Skill v1/2/3, Skill v1/2/3, Skill, Key Word, Key Phrase

Category: Skill v1/2/3, Skill v1/2/3, Skill, Key Word, Key Phrase

THE PROFESSIONAL SUMMARY

Frequently referred to by titles as varying as Summary, Selected Accomplishments, Career Highlights, and Overview, this section is the centerpiece of the first page of your resume. It is designed completely and exclusively to showcase the precise combination of experience, skills, key words, phrases, and accomplishments most likely to attract the attention and focus of your target audience.

In pursuit mode, this will mean highlighting the skills and experiences that make you uniquely qualified for a specific job opening. While positioning to be pursued, you may wish to include additional information that makes you relevant to a broader audience. In both cases, your Professional Summary will be optimized to quickly highlight exactly why you are someone who needs to be contacted right away.

All of the sections on the first page are important, but a Professional Summary is uniquely valuable because of its extreme flexibility. Front-loading aside, the rest of the sections on a resume are usually a bit static. Your education will either be complete and relevant or not, so it will either be present on the first page or not. The same goes for certifications and training. The specific tools, technologies, and key words in your Skills Summary might be reorganized or re-sequenced from time to time, but the overall information generally won't change.

The Professional Summary, however, can be completely and totally different from opportunity to opportunity and job category to job category. It can be adapted to emphasize a variety of skills and experiences, allowing you to build completely distinct and authentic resumes that are optimized for very different hiring audiences. This can be extremely helpful when applying for specific positions or creating Master Resumes designed to target particular job types (more on this shortly).

Here are a few important concepts to keep in mind as you build your own Professional Summary.

- The more important a given piece of information, the closer to the top of your Professional Summary it will go. Remember, you have to speak fast and deliver a focused message to capture the attention of your audience.

- Organize your information into concise bullet points, not long paragraphs or run-on sentences. The information in your Professional Summary has to be easily read and understood. Bullet points help divide distinct concepts and ideas into easy-to-read chunks and make it much easier for you to modify and adjust the key points as appropriate.

- Stay focused on facts, skills, experiences, and achievements while avoiding an excess of opinions and narrative description. Facts are good, opinions can wait.

- Remember that managers generally love to see quantifiable results and tangible outcomes. If a project you worked on saved your company time or money (or helped to generate revenue and profit), make sure that information is included. If you managed a budget or staff, include the dollar amount and team size. If you created a tangible product, website, code snippet, or outcome, mention it.

- Include as many of the relevant key words from your Skills Summary as possible. Resume readers scan for repetition of relevant search terms – if a key phrase shows up only once, most readers will assume it wasn't a big part of your experience. When a word or phrase shows up multiple times it creates an impression that you have a higher degree of expertise (pay attention to this trend as you read through the sample resume content in this section).

- Include at least enough information to capture the attention of your audience and showcase your talents. A Professional Summary should be concise, but not minimalist.

A best practice when building a Professional Summary is to make a giant list of bulleted sentences that capture your most relevant experiences, skills, keywords, and accomplishments. This "meta summary" will grow as your experiences expand, and will serve as a source document for creating customized professional summaries and submittal content whenever you need it (visit www.michaelbjunge.com for examples).

Cutting and pasting from the larger document will enable you to create a first page that is optimized to a very specific opportunity or spot-on for a particular type of position. Rather than writing a new summary every time you apply to a job posting, you can create a customized summary with just a few keystrokes and mouse clicks. Very cool, and very effective.

The professional summary you use on a particular resume shouldn't exceed six or seven highly relevant bullet points, and sometimes three or four will be more than enough. The idea is to be equal parts relevant and efficient, and you definitely don't want the real highlights buried in an avalanche of extraneous information.

FAST TRACK CHALLENGE:

Create a new Professional Summary mimicking the bulleted list format below, highlighting relevant key words and phrases, and adding your own personal touches as desired.

An experienced/expert/accomplished/motivated/dedicated _____ with extensive professional experience and a background that includes:

- **Your strongest and most relevant skills and experience, and the number of years you've spent developing those skills and abilities.** Ideally this will be among your greatest strengths and most marketable skills.
- **Client/employment history.** This should include a quick summary of "name recognition" clients and industry competitors, along with a skill set or achievement gained while working there.
- **Recent project activities that are directly relevant to a specific opportunity or type of opportunity.** One or two things you have done recently that are similar to the needs of the potential employer.
- **Relevant skills and experiences.** Presented in sentence format, highlight all of the specific skills and experience you believe will be useful to the client.
- **Other skills and experiences.** Anything else that may be perceived as a selling point.

WORK EXPERIENCE

By the time a resume reader gets to your Work Experience, they should be itching to pick up the phone and schedule an interview (or send an email, if that's their preferred mode of communication). At this point your primary job is to support the case you have already made by showing exactly *where* and *how* you did all the great things described in the previous sections of your resume.

Whether you choose to call it a Career Summary, Employment History, Work History, or something similar, this part of your resume will be used to showcase the specific tasks and projects you've completed, the experiences and achievements you've enjoyed, and the contributions you've made to past employers. It will also allow you to reinforce, in context, the key words and phrases mentioned in the earlier parts of your resume.

As you format the header for each employer in your Work Experience section, be sure to include the employer name, dates of employment (month and year), and a hybrid title (as described above). In the actual description, follow a similar format to the Professional Summary. Use simple, clear bullet points. Describe your accomplishments in short one and two sentence summaries. Quantify your results. Include the names and version numbers of relevant tools and technologies you've used. As with every other part of your resume, your job is to make it easy for the reader to say yes to you.

ROUGH TRACK RECORD?

If you have a spotty work history, take a moment for a quick reality check. No matter how many tough breaks you've had, your career woes aren't entirely caused by bad bosses or bad luck (and even if some are, dwelling on it won't help you land your next job).

Instead of looking for external causes, focus on identifying your role in the pattern and figure out what to do differently this time around. Own up to one of your shortcomings (i.e. - attitude, work ethic, training, or experience), and share what you've done to overcome that issue.

Nobody is perfect, and people will be far more inclined to give you a shot if they feel you're aware of your own limitations and are working to get better.

Below is a job description template. All of the key elements that made the Skills and Professional Summaries useful are included, along with relevant information about the employer, job duties, and length of stay. You will also note that an "environment" section has been added to the bottom of the description. An environment section allows for further reinforcement of the tools, technologies, skills, and phrases used while working for that specific employer. Including such a summary is a simple, effective way to catch the eye and concisely summarize useful information.

FAST TRACK CHALLENGE:

Create your Work Experience section, starting with your most recent employer. You can use the format outlined below or create a variation of your own. As you build it out, include as much detail as possible. Your description may be longer or shorter than the example depending on your length of stay and level of responsibility, but for the sake of the exercise, capture as much information as you can. Repeat the process for each employer over the past five to ten years.

Start Date-   <u>Company Name</u>
End Date   **Hybrid Title**

Project/Position Summary. Include important details such as team size, budget, key words, purpose, scope, and so on.

- Description of primary tasks and functions carried out in this role.
- Details of exactly what the job entailed, including relevant tools, technologies, methodologies, and other useful key words.
- Information about the nature and scope of your work, including team interactions and personal accountabilities.
- Information about a successful outcome that was produced as a result of your efforts.
- Additional details pertaining to the tasks carried out in the job.
- More bullets and details about exactly what you did and how you did it.
- Other project/position details as relevant.

Environment: Skill v1/2/3, Skill v1/2/3, Skill v1/2/3, Skill v1/2/3, Skill, Key Word, Key Phrase Skill, Key Word, Key Phrase, Tool, Methodology, Other.

BUILDING A MASTER RESUME (OR MASTER RESUMES)

You've created the primary elements that comprise an attention grabbing resume and begun the process of building out the content that will comprise your final resume(s). Now it's time to roll up your sleeves and finish out the process. If you are only going to pursue one type of job, a single resume will probably be adequate and you can power your way through the rest of your

Work Experience section (but do a round or two of proofreading and editing before you really call it a wrap).

If you intend to apply for multiple types of positions, however, it's a good idea to have multiple versions of your resume, each customized to speak to a specific audience or type of opportunity. That's where master resumes come in.

A master resume is a highly optimized document that will focus on the unique set of skills and experiences that will be relevant to a particular hiring audience. It is a version of your resume designed to attract resume readers with a precise set of hiring needs, and will use specific keyword criteria in their candidate search process.

An individual who has worked in a pre-sales engineering position, for example, might have one resume that is optimized for sales openings, another for IT or engineering, and a third for consulting positions. Although all versions of the resume would share a great deal of content, each would have a different emphasis and construction, especially in the Professional Summary section.

In every case, the details that are most relevant to a given audience will be highlighted and moved to the front, and each master resume will include a customized Skills Summary and Professional Summary (and possibly a customized Work Experience section as well) designed to cater to an audience with unique hiring needs. The goal is to cover everything you've ever done that might be relevant to that particular type of employer—academically, professionally, and on a volunteer basis.

These variations on your resume will target completely different audiences and be seen by completely different people. And don't worry – writing customized or "niche" specific resumes is an accepted industry practice. Even if the same person sees two different versions of your resume (which won't happen often if you follow the guidelines in this book), the odds are good that the only questions they'll ask are regarding the congruence and accuracy of the information presented. Provided everything is genuine, you're on solid ground and can explain that you are targeting two different types of jobs and emphasizing different aspects of your experience for each. No big deal.

The process of creating these resumes serves a number of purposes. Each master resume functions as a source document from which to pull information and create more focused resumes "on demand." This is especially useful when proactively submitting your resume to specific opportunities, an activity that requires an even more detailed level of customization and is completely distinct from posting a resume and waiting for responses.

Another great benefit of creating multiple versions of your resume is that it will force you to remember all of the different things you've done and organize them in your own mind. It provides a great opportunity to reflect on past successes and failures, remember the people you've worked with, and gain clarity about what you've learned and accomplished as a professional.

The more clearly you organize the information in your mind, the more effective you will be at articulating it in your next interview. Great interviewers are able to respond instantly to questions about their background and experience. They don't have to hesitate and think about what they did or how they did it. They just know. This process will help you get to that point. And let's face it, the last thing you want to say when someone asks you a question about your own background is, "Ummm. Hmmmm. Uhhh. Welllll...Let me think about that." It's your own experience for crying out loud. You'd better know it inside and out.

As you go through the upcoming exercise, consider taking it to another level by writing down the name of every person you worked with at each employer, along with what they did, how your roles were related, and whether or not they'd be a good reference. This takes time, but will be very helpful with several of the practices prescribed later in this book.

If you've worked in multiple positions within the same organization or been involved in multiple projects, treat each position or project as a distinct entity and document it separately (within the realm of reason, of course...even master resumes can't be a hundred pages long).

FAST TRACK CHALLENGE:

Complete the process of creating at least one master resume – using either this format or another. Provided you achieve the purpose of delivering useful information quickly, the style can be altered at will.

Full Name

Contact Details

Education (if relevant):

Degree, Institution (GPA if outstanding) - Date of Completion

Degree, Institution (GPA if outstanding) - Date of Completion

Training (if relevant):

Type of Training, Company/Institution - Date of Completion

Certification (if relevant):

Name of Certification, Certifying Body - Date of Completion

Skills Summary:

Category: Skill v1/2/3, Skill v1/2/3, Skill, Key Word, Key Phrase

Category: Skill v1/2/3, Skill v1/2/3, Skill, Key Word, Key Phrase

Category: Skill v1/2/3, Skill v1/2/3, Skill, Key Word, Key Phrase

Category: Skill v1/2/3, Skill v1/2/3, Skill, Key Word, Key Phrase

Category: Skill v1/2/3, Skill v1/2/3, Skill, Key Word, Key Phrase

PROFESSIONAL SUMMARY:

An experienced/expert/accomplished/motivated/dedicated _____ with extensive professional experience and a background that includes:

- **A bullet about your strongest and most relevant skills and experience, preferably referencing the number of years you've spent developing them into talents.** Ideally this will be directly relevant to target employers and among your most marketable skills.

- **Client/employment history.** This should include a quick summary of employers (ideally including at least one "name recognition" client), along with a skill set or achievement gained while working at these companies.
- **Recent project activities directly relevant to a specific opportunity or type of opportunity.** One or two things you have done recently that are similar to the needs of the potential employer.
- **Relevant skills and experiences.** In sentence format, highlight all of the specific skills and experience you believe will be useful to the client.
- **Other skills and experiences** that may be perceived as a selling point.

Work Experience:

Start Date-   <u>Company Name</u>
End Date   **Hybrid Title**

Project/Position Summary. Include important details such as team size, budget, key words, purpose, scope, and so on.

- Description of primary tasks and functions carried out in this role.
- Details of exactly what the job entailed, including relevant tools, technologies, methodologies, and other useful key words.
- Information about the nature and scope of your work, including team interactions and personal accountabilities.
- Information about a successful outcome that was produced as a result of your efforts.
- Additional details pertaining to the tasks carried out in the job.
- More bullets and details about exactly what you did and how you did it.
- Other project/position details as relevant.

Environment: Skill v1/2/3, Skill v1/2/3, Skill v1/2/3, Skill v1/2/3, Skill, Key Word, Key Phrase Skill, Key Word, Key Phrase, Tool, Methodology, Other.

Start Date-   <u>Company Name #2</u>
End Date   **Hybrid Title**

Repeat format from above, with the option of including fewer bullets and slightly less content. Start with a simple Project/Position Summary and include important details such as team size, budget, key words, purpose, scope, and so on.

- One bullet description of the primary tasks and functions carried out in this role.

- Additional details of exactly what the job entailed, including relevant tools, technologies, methodologies, and other useful key words.

- Information about the nature and scope of your work, including team interactions and personal accountabilities.

- Information about a successful outcome that resulted from your efforts.

- Additional details, relevant information, and other project/position details as relevant.

Environment: Skill v1/2/3, Skill v1/2/3, Skill v1/2/3, Skill v1/2/3, Skill, Key Word, Key Phrase Skill, Key Word, Key Phrase, Tool, Methodology, Other.

NOW WHAT?

Two things. First, continue building master resumes until you've created one for each type of opportunity you actively wish to pursue. That sets you up for the next step – making sure you put the right resume in the right places and attracting the right people. That's key.

Second, take a minute and make sure the voicemail message on your primary phone line is "business ready." You are probably not going to be around to answer every call that comes in - even if it's a cell number you've provided - and a lame or unprofessional message (i.e. - "whazzzupppppp") could easily turn off an otherwise interested employer.

If you're not sure what to say, keep it short, sweet, and to the point. Consider something to the effect of "Hi you've reached _____. I'm sorry I'm not here to take your call right now, but if you leave your name, number, and a brief message I'll get back to you as soon I can. Thanks for calling, and have a great day!"

GETTING MAGNETIC

"When you can do the common things of life in an uncommon way, you will command the attention of the world."

George Washington Carver

Once you're finished building out your resume(s) and updating your voicemail, it's time to start attracting attention from the three primary hiring audiences (recruiters, HR professionals, and hiring managers). That means posting your resume in the places where these audiences are searching for people with your skills and experience.

A number of online venues are used by resume readers across almost all industries and job segments. CareerBuilder, Monster, HotJobs, and LinkedIn are among the leaders in multi-industry resume posting and candidate search, and it's a good idea to leverage all of them.

Beyond the major job boards, there are countless niche sites designed to serve more specific markets, including major players such as Dice.com (information technology) and BioSpace (biotech and pharmaceutical). If you aren't familiar with the niche sites in your field, run a quick Google search or check in with your Groups on LinkedIn (more on this later). If you have a niche skill set, it's a great idea to get your profile posted in the places where people with niche requirements go looking for talent.

Given the ways most search engines work, there are a couple simple tricks you can use to maximize visibility and minimize conflicts or confusion over the various versions of your resume being posted.

1) Post only one version of your resume per site at a given time. It's okay to use multiple versions of your resume on the same source, but given that search engines use date and key word criteria to determine which results to display and in which order, a separation of a few days between postings is a good idea.

2) Refresh each resume on a weekly or bi-weekly basis (the methods for updating vary from site to site, but the majority make it as easy as clicking a button and don't require updating the content). Most resume searchers use date parameters to narrow down the volume of results returned by a given query, and many only look at resumes that have been updated within the past few days or weeks.

3) On sites that allow only a single version of your resume or profile (such as LinkedIn, Plaxo, or a personal web page), use the one that represents the type of job you are most interested in landing. Load this up with lots of relevant key words and detail to make sure you draw as large an audience as possible. You may also want to consider using a larger than normal professional summary to highlight a broader range of skills and experiences (eight to ten bullets instead of four to six).

FAST TRACK CHALLENGE:

Post your resume on at least one major job board (Monster, CareerBuilder, HotJobs, etc), and one niche resume site. Start today, using the version of your resume that represents the type of opportunity you most want to land.

SUBMITTING WITH STYLE

Although it is the most time consuming and painful of the prescribed methods for securing interviews, proactively responding to job postings is nonetheless useful. Unlike posting and blasting, submitting your resume allows you to go after specific positions and employers that you find particularly appealing. Response rates to on-line resume submittals tend to be really low, so there is huge value in knowing how to effectively pursue and land the jobs you identify without going down that path.

The first rule is DO NOT SUBMIT YOUR RESUME THROUGH A JOB BOARD OR COMPANY WEBSITE – not unless it is requested by a recruiter or human resources professional.

Sending unsolicited resumes is usually a waste of energy, and there are better ways to spend your time (unless you like the feeling of banging your head into the wall). Instead, consider investing the time required to identify the person in charge of recruiting for the position and sending them your resume directly. It takes longer, but the difference in response rates is staggering. A simple but exceptionally effective process is to search LinkedIn for the name of a recruiter or human resources professional at the hiring organization, call the company phone number, and ask for the specific person by name.

To find a person on LinkedIn, go to the People search (looks like a Google search bar), type in the name of the company and add the words "talent acquisition," "recruiter," or "recruiting." Most of the time you'll find the name of least one person in the Recruiting or HR department, and then it's simply a matter of visiting the company website or 411.com to find the phone number.

Once you've reached a human being, let them know the title or specific requisition number for the position you found and ask for their email address. Even if they aren't in charge of recruiting for that particular position, they'll usually let you know who is or accept your resume and pass it along to the right person. Either way, your odds of getting a real response go way, way up.

The next question is what to do after making contact. Submitting a resume requires a little more effort and finesse than attracting attention on the job boards. As Mary demonstrated, it pays to optimize the entire submittal to grab the attention of your target audience. Time invested in constructing an outstanding resume submittal is often paid off with a speedier response and a higher rate of interview requests. Here are a few guidelines for putting together a tail-kicking submittal:

1) Customize the Subject Line to reflect the needs of the hiring organization. Your name is far less relevant than your skill set (at this point anyway). A best practice is to use a subject line that includes the Job Title and one or two key words from the job description rather than any personal identification or content (i.e. Expert Software Developer with 10+ Years of Accounting Systems Experience).

break it up

2) Include a brief introductory email that focuses entirely on the aspects of your background that are relevant to this specific position. Open with a pleasant introductory sentence, add two or three bullet points loaded with keywords and related experience, and close with a call to action or expression of gratitude.

3) Briefly customize the version of your Master Resume that is most closely aligned to the specific position. Use Hybrid Titles and adjust the order and sequence of the information in each section to highlight the most relevant keywords and content.

4) Attach Letters of Recommendation and Work Samples as applicable and appropriate. Only use those that reflect excellence and are directly relevant to your target audience.

5) Copy yourself on each resume submittal and archive the emails where they can be easily found. This will ensure that you have access to the version of the resume sent to each specific client, and will also allow you to borrow the content for future submittals to positions of a similar nature.

FAST TRACK CHALLENGE:

Before the end of today, make contact with at least one recruiter (or talent acquisition specialist, as they sometimes prefer to be called) at a company with a relevant job opening. Once you've made contact, send a clean, professional submittal directly to their email address.

Bonus Points:

Pick a Resume Blaster and use it to send your favorite resume out to the market at large. Use the same parameters discussed in Submitting with Style (a customized subject line, brief introductory email, and lots of relevant keywords).

THE ART OF INTERVIEWING LIKE A PRO

"(it) has nothing to do with what you are expecting to get —
only what you are expecting to give — which is everything."

Katharine Hepburn

❦

E ven before we met it was clear that Greg was different from the average job seeker. For starters, he seemed excited about the prospect of meeting with me, a relatively junior recruiter, to further discuss the opportunity described in our initial conversation. In a down market that might not seem strange, but this was February of 2000, and the market was still riding the high of the tech bubble. Certified IT Project Managers with a legitimate professional track record had their pick of opportunities, and most treated recruiters as a nuisance (or worse). A receptive audience was something of an oddity.

The positive attitude actually raised red flags in my mind, and I half-expected Greg to flake on our scheduled meeting. Two minutes before our 11 a.m. appointment time, however, my phone rang and the receptionist let me know I had a guest in the lobby. I walked out and found an impeccably dressed man beaming an enormous smile in my direction. It was impossible not to return the gesture as we shook hands and exchanged pleasantries. By the time we walked back to the interviewing room I was already off my guard and completely at ease.

As we sat down, Greg pulled out a copy of his resume and a big black binder. He handed me the resume and set the binder off to one side. The binder piqued my curiosity, but I started into my structured interview routine as normal. I shared about myself and the firm I represented, set expectations for how the interview would go, and opened the floor for questions. He asked exactly one: "Can you tell me a little more about the opportunity and exactly what you're looking for in terms of skills and experience?"

I shared a brief overview of the position and my understanding of what a successful applicant would bring to the table. I asked if he had any other questions but he just smiled and said, "No, that sounds great. Fire away."

As we progressed through a standard series of questions about his skill set and background, I found myself amazed at how perfectly "on target" Greg was for the opportunity in question. It was as if he were tailor-made for the position. I found myself growing more and more excited about the difference he could make for our client and how great I was going to look for finding him.

As we got deeper into the interview I started to dig into the specific details of his projects and ask more pointed questions about the nature of the work he did. Greg reached to the side of the table and grabbed the big black binder. For the next thirty minutes he blew my socks off by showcasing a series of project plans, documents, and testimonials the likes of which I'd never seen before. He didn't just talk the talk and he didn't expect me to take on faith that he walked the walk. He had beautifully documented proof that he was exactly what he claimed to be and more.

By the end of our conversation I didn't just want our client to hire Greg. I wanted to commission him as an exhibit for the museum of awesomeness. The guy was just plain fantastic! Later that day we submitted his resume to our client along with two letters of recommendation and one sample project plan from his portfolio. Within hours the client responded, eager to bring him in for an interview.

Three days and four interviews later we received an offer for Greg that was more than 10 percent higher than the "top end" of the salary range our client had given at the beginning of the search process. We didn't even have to negotiate. The CIO was positive Greg was the right candidate and wanted to make sure no one else scooped him up. Two weeks later he started his new job, and a year later he brought in one of the first "on-time, under budget" software implementations in the history of the organization. Today Greg runs the company. Literally.

"Wise men talk because they have something to say;
fools talk because they have to say something."

Plato

As Greg so aptly demonstrated in our first meeting, there's both an art and science to interviewing. Over the course of our relationship it came out that he had a great deal of depth and experience he DIDN'T discuss in that first interview. He knew that he would have ample opportunity to showcase his other skills if he landed the position, and that by staying focused on the needs of the client, he was far more likely to be in a position to make that happen.

Focusing on the needs of others is one of the first secrets to mastering the interview process and landing great opportunities. This section exposes a handful of the tactics used by industry insiders to beat out the competition, along with techniques picked up from real-world interview experts like Greg. Most can be applied immediately and with very little difficulty, while others require an investment of time and repetition before they develop into practical skills.

Every company and team has slightly different hiring practices, but the overall interview process can be broken down into a few common and distinct components. Each provides opportunities to add value, stand out from the competition, and put yourself in position to land a great offer. Everything starts with preparation. After that it's all about the first impression, transition, interview body, closing, and follow-up.

Each component of the interview will be addressed separately, allowing you to test and explore the various strategies individually or in combination. As you progress, don't worry about applying every new idea immediately. It is far more important to appear genuine in an interview than to have a dozen fancy techniques at your disposal. Focus on the practices you find most relevant and comfortable. Make an effort to master two or three, and ignore everything that doesn't seem to fit for you.

The information included in this section is intended to help you bring the best of yourself to the interview. The goal of leveraging these strategies is not to trick someone into hiring you, but rather to provide an expanded sense of confidence and the opportunity to deliver real value to those conducting the interview.

GETTING PREPARED

First things first. If you're going to ace an interview you have to be prepared. Every interview is unique and will present a distinct set of challenges and opportunities, but there are a handful of universally useful ways to effectively prepare for a professional interview. These can be considered general guidelines and have practical value regardless of your level of experience. Most are applicable even if you are interviewing for a promotion or new job within your current company and want a leg up on the competition. In short, these practices can and should be followed each and every time you get ready to interview.

- Do Your Homework on the Company
- Review the Position Description
- Review Your Own Skills and Experiences
- Practice, Practice, Practice

DO YOUR HOMEWORK ON THE COMPANY

These days you can find out a great deal about almost any company from the comfort of home. Search engines, public forums, chat rooms, company websites, and blogs provide a wealth of information on the majority of companies in the English-speaking world. Depending on your current level as a professional, some pieces of information will be more relevant and applicable than others.

If you are interviewing for an executive job, for example, it would be wise to have a firm grasp of the financial status of the organization, and a clear understanding of the mission, vision, goals, and values that guide the direction of the company in general. Publicly traded companies typically have annual and quarterly financial statements, news releases, articles, and executive profiles available online, providing a huge amount of relevant and useful information for the proactive job seeker.

You might also want to track down executive profiles (on the company website and/or LinkedIn), press releases (company website and/or search engine query), and explicitly relevant information on the company website. You could take it a step further and check in discussion boards, forums, and blogs to see what others are saying, but bear in mind that the loudest and most vocal contributors aren't typically the happily employed.

At an entry level it might be sufficient to know some basic information about the organization (company website), the products and services they provide (company website, search engine query), and gain a general sense of the culture and environment (company website, social networking sites, or a quick call to the receptionist).

For bonus points – and a significant competitive advantage - visit www. glassdoor.com. The site is an online venue where anonymous employees and past interviewees post interesting and relevant information about the hiring practices and work environments of countless companies (including specific interview questions). There are over 950 interview questions and reviews posted about Google alone, and even more on a number of larger employers.

REVIEW THE SPECIFIC POSITION DESCRIPTION

When interviewing and applying for a number of different opportunities, eventually you're going to lose track of which requirements pertain to each specific job. Unless you literally have a photographic memory, you'll want a backup system in place to make sure you're preparing for the right position each time you interview. A simple practice is to create an email folder called "job openings" or "resume submittals" and use it to archive relevant position descriptions and the resume submitted for each one.

If you lose or forget to archive the details of a given position, it can usually be tracked down with relative ease. These days almost every position comes with a written job description that is posted in multiple places online, and that description is probably what prompted you to send a resume or agree to take an interview in the first place.

Search Indeed.com, the major job boards, or the company website to find the description without human interaction, or call HR and ask for a copy if you can't find it any other way. The written description is only a starting point, but it can help you identify "hot buttons," key points of interest, and areas where you might need to spend a little time reviewing prior to your interview.

REVIEW YOUR OWN RESUME AND BACKGROUND

The primary value of having a written job description to work from is that it allows you to identify the strengths that make you qualified and the gaps that could make you look weak or incapable. Having a firm grasp of both can be a critical differentiator in an interview race between comparably qualified candidates. Everything on your resume is fair game, and even the smallest phrase or key word can be an opening for detailed probing questions.

As you prepare to interview, there are three basic areas on which to focus: your strengths, weaknesses, and experience as a whole. The third is the easiest and will allow you to more effectively approach the first two.

A great place to start is with a review of your resume. Specifically, you should look over the content of the exact resume you posted or submitted, and make sure to have copies of that version printed out and available when you go in to the interview.

Next, do a brief review of the aspects of the job description fall into the other categories – strength and weakness. Take the time to go beyond the surface level. Don't just look at the description and say, "I've got that handled." How do you have it handled? What specifically have you done that makes you qualified? What have you learned that might be valuable to a prospective employer? What *similar* skills and experience do you bring to the table that might also be relevant? You should be ready, willing, and able to speak confidently and comfortably about your past successes and failures, and know them well enough to have the conversation be meaningful to the other person.

Addressing weaknesses and gaps in your experience will help mitigate the negative impact these might have on the confidence of your audience. The first step is to identify them as "weaknesses." Don't gloss over them and don't expect to rely exclusively on your strengths to land the opportunity. That's not always good enough. You need to anticipate that the gaps will be on the mind of the hiring authority and proactively prepare to address them.

There are many ways to present weaknesses as strengths and minimize the damaging effects of "not having experience" in a given area (several effective techniques will be presented in the "overcoming objections" section just ahead). An important point is to remember that the hiring manager is primarily going to be interested in how you can help solve a problem or help produce a desired result—not all the cool things you've done that are totally unrelated to their requirements.

The more articulate you are about your own skills and experience and the more clear you are about how your skills and experience relate to a given position, the more likely you are to deliver value to the person interviewing you. At the end of the day, that's the thing that's most likely to help you land the position.

When it comes time to interview, you should be prepared to speak articulately about every job you've done, every team you've worked on, and every aspect of your skill set and experience. If it's on your resume, you have to own it. That means being clear about your strengths, comfortable addressing your weaknesses, and prepared to speak about any aspect of your background that happens to come up in the conversation.

PRACTICE, PRACTICE, PRACTICE

"It's a funny thing, the more I practice the luckier I get."

Arnold Palmer

The old adage "practice makes perfect" may not be one hundred percent accurate, but it's a solid reminder that there's huge value in putting in the leg work. Unlike areas where the rewards may be intangible, the benefits of mastering the interview process can be directly translated into dollars and cents (and that always a strong motivator).

So how does one practice interviewing? As it turns out, lots of ways. You can download a list of tough interview questions from the internet and practice responding to them in your free time. You can write a monologue describing exactly what you did on your most recent project and practice speaking it out loud. You can identify a few of the specific accomplishments and tangible results you've produced and share about them with a friend or significant other.

If you want to take things to the next level, there are a variety of techniques and strategies that can help you kick your game up a notch. Those reviewed in this section are commonly used by professional speakers and presenters, and can be highly effective in polishing and sharpening your presentation skills.

1. Practice speaking in front of a mirror. This may sound a bit corny, but talking in front of a mirror is one of the simplest, cheapest (free), and most effective ways to improve presentation skills known to man. As you watch yourself speaking, you receive real-time feedback about your

posture, facial expression, confidence, and delivery. And let's face it… you're your own toughest critic. If you can get yourself excited about hiring you, everyone else should be relatively easy to persuade.

2. Find a mentor or advisor who has experience conducting interviews and ask them to give you a thorough grilling (friend, family member, past boss, etc). Arm them with a list of the questions you LEAST want to answer, and ask them to attack you with them. The more comfortable you get handling tough questions in a practice setting, the more likely you are to ace them in a real life situation.

3. Videotape yourself talking about your background, work experience, and skills. Get yourself on camera responding to tough interview questions, introducing yourself, or just plain talking. Just like practicing in front of a mirror, video provides an exceptional opportunity to evaluate your own strengths and weaknesses and get direct feedback on where to improve. The added benefit of video is that it allows a more detailed analysis and the opportunity to review your performance multiple times.

All of these methods provide unique insight and valuable opportunities to improve. A solid mentor will give you honest feedback and direct advice. Friends and family will give you the chance to practice and rehearse in front of an audience. A video camera will allow you to self-assess from a uniquely first and third person perspective all at the same time. A mirror will force you to be present while also providing instant feedback from your own toughest critic.

Start with one or two of these methods for now, and consider working with all of them over the next few months. Make a game of the process. Practice the way an athlete or musician practices their craft, with the dual intention of getting better and having fun. Interviewing may be serious business, but it doesn't have to feel seriously stressful. The more you prepare, the better you will perform. The better you perform, the more fun you have and the greater your chances of getting hired.

MAKING A GREAT FIRST IMPRESSION

"The beginning is the most important part of the work."

Plato

An interview, like a book, is made up of three fundamental components – an opening, body, and conclusion. Each represents an opportunity to distinguish oneself from the competition and make a uniquely positive impression. Starting strong provides the distinct advantage of shading everything else that happens in a positive light. Greg demonstrated this principle with remarkable style and class – he had me completely at ease and confident in his interpersonal skills before we ever sat down to interview.

The way you start the interview dictates the feeling and flow of everything that follows. As it turns out, setting a great tone is relatively easy. It requires only that you be able to 1) dress appropriately 2) offer a genuine smile, 3) give a firm, dry handshake, and 4) say "thank you" to the person who is conducting the interview.

This may seem too simple to work, but that's the way it is with the fundamentals. They're basic, and they work. This simple approach can easily make the difference between a positive connection and a mundane or perfunctory interview process (especially if the smile and appreciation are genuine). That's not to say it's impossible to turn things around if you get off to a rocky start or can't pull together a winning introduction. Far from it. It is to say that it's far preferable (and a great deal more enjoyable) to get off to a good start in the first place.

In an in-person interview a good general rule is to "dress a level up." A three piece suit isn't appropriate attire at a surf shop, and flip flops and board shorts won't cut it on Wall Street. Know your audience and dress a little bit better than would be expected in your day to day job. When in doubt, call the receptionist or an HR representative for advice.

Looking good and wearing the right clothes should help you find confidence, but nerves are still likely to play a role the first time you walk into a

Phone Interview?

Just as books often include a preface, many hiring processes also involve at least one phone interview. A priceless tip for phone interviews is to imagine that the person is in the same room as you and smile as if you were standing face to face. The shape of your mouth changes the tone of your voice, which literally makes your smile travel right through the phone.

new environment. A great technique for starting an interview on the right note is to greet the interviewer with the same sort of smile and energy you'd give an old friend. Making the other person feel fantastic is the best possible way to start an interview and not all that hard to do.

If you struggle with sweaty palms and worry about giving a dry handshake, keep a handkerchief in your hand and your hand in your pocket until the last possible moment. Emotion is 10% body and 90% mind. The exact same feeling in your body can be interpreted as anxiety or excitement. Treat those butterflies in your stomach as excitement, and you can immediately transform from nervous into confident and enthusiastic (but don't forget that handkerchief...excitement can cause sweaty palms too).

TRANSITIONING LIKE A PRO

"A gossip is someone who talks to you about others, a bore is someone who talks to you about himself, and a brilliant conversationalist is one who talks to you about yourself."

Lisa Kirk

When Greg asked the question, "Can you tell me a little more about the opportunity and exactly what skills and experience the right candidate will possess?" he was setting up a transition that would empower him to ace the rest of the interview process. The question was deliberate, intentional, and brilliant. After setting a positive tone for the interview by making a great first impression, that's the next step in mastering the interview process—finding out what's important to the other person. Since no two people will have exactly the same perception about a given role or opportunity, asking is the only sure-fire way to find out what's important to each individual interviewer.

By asking the question and taking the time to listen to my perspective, Greg was able to customize his approach to the entire interview to highlight the skills and experiences that were most relevant to me. He did exactly the same thing with each of the interviewers at our end client. This meant that everyone he met felt as though he or she had been listened to (hugely important), and even better, that Greg fit their perception of what the right candidate would bring to the table.

He wasn't being sneaky or disingenuous. He was being very, very smart. Greg possessed all of the skills and experiences that he presented in his interviews in spades. What he didn't do was waste time and energy sharing aspects of his background and experience that weren't relevant to his target audience. Sadly, this is where most people spend the majority of their interview hours— talking about things that are irrelevant to the other party and carrying the conversation in directions that help nobody. Don't do that.

Your goal is to set up a highly effective interview, and the best way to do that is to make sure you focus your attention on the right things. You find out what the right things are by asking the right person – the one who is interviewing you – what it is that they're looking for. This must happen at the BEGINNING of the interview. Key point. Waiting to find out what's important on your way out the door is pretty much useless.

At the beginning of your next interview, try one of the following phrases or create a variation of your own:

"I've done some research on the opportunity already, but would love to hear in your words what skills and experiences the right candidate will possess."

"I'd love to talk about my background, but before I do, would you mind sharing your goals for this position? I'd like to make sure I keep my responses focused on things that are going to be relevant to you and your team."

"Can you tell me what skills and attributes would make someone successful in this role?"

"What skills and experiences would make a candidate qualified for this position?"

"Can you tell me a little more about the goals and purpose of this position?"

"Would you mind sharing your perspective on which of the skills and experiences listed in the job description will be the most important and relevant to this opportunity?"

> "My recruiter shared some of the basic details about this opportunity, but I'd love to hear in your own words what it is that you're looking to accomplish."

Be appropriate to the situation, and feel free to customize, modify, or make up a similar question that works with your own personality and comfort level. The important thing is to ASK the other person what they are looking for and LISTEN to their response, and to do both at the *beginning* of the interview.

THE BODY

"Know thyself."

Socrates

The transition will set you up for success by making the rest of the interview relevant to the listener. That's the first secret to interview success, and if that's the only thing you learn from this section, you're already way ahead of the competition. What comes next is the interview body, which comprises the majority of the conversation. Not only does the interview body take the most time, it is also the part that offers the most potential variance and greatest opportunity to develop genuine rapport.

The keys to being effective at this stage of the game revolve around the ability to articulate your skills and experiences, responding to questions in a logical and cohesive way, overcoming potential issues, and addressing challenges that might affect your candidacy. Each topic is highlighted and addressed below.

DEMONSTRATING SELF-KNOWLEDGE AND CONVERSATION FLUENCY

In the hiring process it is useful to remember that you are both the product and the sales person. The better you know yourself and what you have to offer, the easier it is for your audience to recognize your value as a resource.

Once you get past the transition there are two levels of expertise you can demonstrate in articulating your own skills and experience. The first was covered in the section on preparation and is the ability to speak with confidence about the things you've done and the skills you have gained as a professional (or student, if you are newly entering the workforce). The second is communicating these skills and experiences in a way that specifically relates to the goals and objectives of the interviewer.

When you walk into an interview, you should be exceptionally well-prepared to speak, explain, and expand on who you are and what you've done as a professional. It's your career, resume, and experience, and you have to be prepared to talk about it with confidence. Perhaps even more important is to listen to the goals and objectives of the interviewer so you can share the experiences and qualifications that enable you to be of service.

The process of developing a higher level of self-knowledge and conversational fluency began when you created your master resume. Reviewing your professional background and related experiences at a detailed level is a key part of the equation and will help ensure that you are able to talk effectively about things that are relevant to the interviewer. Among the most important areas to cover are:

- Each project you worked on and each task you performed.
- The purpose and goal of each project and task (i.e. - the desired outcome or reason for doing the task in the first place).
- The names and roles of the people on your team—subordinates, peers,

managers, and partners.

- The tools, technologies, methodologies, and approaches you used.
- The results that were actually accomplished through your efforts.

Ideally you'll also be able to quantify the results of your efforts in terms of dollars and/or tangible end products, but unless you work at a management level consider that to be extra credit.

---

*"Most of the successful people I've known are the ones
who do more listening than talking."*

Bernard M. Baruch

After refreshing your knowledge of your own skills and experience you will have a much easier time accomplishing the second level of conversational fluency—the ability to communicate those skills and experiences in relation to the wants and needs of your audience. This is the level that separates an expert from an amateur. Getting to that point is completely dependent on the ability to ask targeted questions and listen attentively to the answers. A simple but and highly effective model for moving into the category of expert is:

Ask → Listen → Summarize → Respond

In an interview, the first targeted question you should ask is some variation on "What skills and experience will the right candidate possess?" or "What specific goals and objectives are you hoping to achieve through filling this position?" If you listen closely to the answer, the other person will often hand over the blueprint for acing the interview.

To be certain you've understood what the person actually intended, summarize and confirm what they have said. That's the only way to be sure that your interpretation is correct and in alignment with their intention. A great way to do that is use a phrase like:

> "If I understand you correctly, the key skills and attributes you are looking for are…"

> "Okay, great. You're looking for a resource who can do X, Y, and Z. Is that right?"

> "It sounds like your goal is to accomplish ___. Is that on target?"

Taking the time to clarify both the content and the intention of the response minimizes the risk of miscommunication and misunderstanding. We've all had the experience of hearing one thing when the person meant something else, or saying one thing and having the other person respond as though we said something totally different. It happens. You just don't want it to happen in a potentially career-changing interview.

Once you have a clear understanding of what's important to the other person you can begin to formulate your dialogue in a meaningful way. The more effectively you connect your skills and experiences to THEM achieving their goals, the more likely you are to move forward and generate a second-round interview or job offer.

FAST TRACK CHALLENGE:

Create one key question and one key phrase that you will use to help identify and summarize the goals of the next interviewer you meet.

USING STRUCTURED RESPONSES

Your skills and qualifications are going to be evaluated in an interview. That's a given. Experienced interviewers will also use the interview as an opportunity to analyze your thought process. Many consider the ability to respond intelligently to challenging and off-the-wall questions as important as overt qualifications and will ask tough questions solely for the purpose of testing you. In these situations they aren't nearly as interested in what you say as they are in how you think, act, and respond under pressure (though what you say is still pretty important).

Experts are looking to see you demonstrate a level head and the ability to follow a logical process when you formulate a response. An interviewer may ask a question like, "Tell me about the most difficult person you've ever worked with and how you were able to be effective interacting with them." They may genuinely want to hear your story and be curious about what you have to say. More than likely, they'll be even more focused on the way you respond than the content of your response.

Even though there isn't a "right" or "wrong" answer in these situations, there are more and less effective ways of responding. More effective is to demonstrate a logical progression of thought and a clear resolution. Less effective is to tell a rambling story without a clear purpose or conclusion.

An effective response will include a concise summary or overview of the situation, the approach you followed and why, and the eventual outcome. One might respond to the question about a challenging coworker like this:

That's a great question. You know, when I first started at my last company I spent three months working side by side with an engineer who had a bad attitude and disruptive personality. The guy was really smart, but intrusive and a bit sarcastic. He constantly interrupted my focus with irrelevant comments and off-color jokes, and it interfered with my ability to get my job done.

Since we were part of the same team and had to work together, I wanted to resolve the situation as amicably as possible. Instead of going to management I took him aside one afternoon and asked to have a conversation in private. When we talked I let him know that the disruptions were having a negative impact on my performance, and asked that he not interrupt when I was engaged in productive activity.

At first he was a little angry, but by the end of the conversation we agreed that I would put up a 'busy' sign when I was in the middle of an important task and he would respect my privacy during that time. Things were tense at first, but he honored our agreement and I made a point of not leaving the sign up all the time. After a few weeks things loosened up and I invited him out for happy hour as a way to say thanks. Once we'd gotten past that initial rough patch the guy softened up and became a bit of a mentor — at least on the engineering side. We still keep in touch today.

This is a "sunshiny" outcome, but it doesn't have to work out that way for your response to be effective. Remember, it's not just the specific content that's being evaluated; it's also the ability to concisely define the situation, demonstrate an intelligent pathway to a resolution, and articulate a clear outcome—positive or negative.

Sometimes sharing a failure is the best ways to disarm a guarded interviewer and help them trust you. While everyone else is pretending to be perfect, you can expose a weakness and demonstrate the ability to learn and grow all at the same time. You have to be careful with this tactic, but done right, it can put you in a completely different category than your competition.

ANTICIPATE AND OVERCOME OBJECTIONS

"An objection is not a rejection; it is simply a request for more information."

Bo Bennett

Regardless of your qualifications and regardless of how well an interviewer appears to be responding to you, there are usually at least a few challenges to overcome in the interview process. The issue may be a gap in employment, the particulars of your salary history, the size of the companies you've worked for, the short duration of a given project, the lack of a specific certification or training course, an issue relating to your work history, or any of a thousand other things.

In all likelihood you already know exactly what objections a potential employer will have in regards to hiring you. You probably don't even have to look at your resume to figure out what these concerns may be; they define the very questions you hope DON'T get asked during your interview. Whether these issues come out in the interview or not, they are extremely likely to influence a hiring decision. Overtly or subtly, the issues you don't want to deal with will have an impact on whether or not you land a given opportunity.

Some people will tell you to play it by ear and only worry about overcoming the objections that surface during the course of an interview. That's one way to go about it. Others prefer a more proactive approach.

Those who take things head-on know that if there's a major issue on their mind, there's a very good chance it will be on the mind of their interviewer as well. At the end of the day, unspoken objections are far more damaging than the ones that come up in conversation. The overt concerns can be addressed. The others can't.

If you honestly aren't sure what objections you might face, start by looking at this list of common deal killers:

> Your compensation, current or desired, doesn't match the pay range.
> You have gaps in employment history or are currently unemployed.
> You have a shaky job history and/or poor job stability.
> You are over or under qualified for the position.
> You haven't worked with a specific tool or technology.
> You lack a required skill set or type of work experience.
> You haven't worked in the right industry or type of company.
> You don't have a viable motivation for changing employer.

Each of these objections can cut both ways. You can make too much money and intimidate a potential employer, or too little and have them concerned about your depth of skill and experience. You can be perceived as a job hopper on the one hand, or someone who has gotten stuck at the same employer for too long on the other. You can be missing too many relevant skills, or you can have a background that matches so directly that there's no perceived opportunity for growth.

No one has a perfect resume or background, so don't worry about being perfect and don't work too hard to avoid the issues. Instead, take initiative and confront challenges pleasantly and directly. You can think of this "going there first." Going there first means identifying potential objections and addressing them proactively. Done correctly, this approach can mitigate or eliminate the concern and give you a chance to move beyond the issue and into the next phase of the conversation.

As you might imagine, there is a delicate balance to maintain when following the "go there first" methodology. While you absolutely DO want to proactively address potential objections and concerns, you absolutely DON'T want to spend the entire interview on issues or come across as defensive or confrontational. A direct, open, and honest approach is best. Here are a few examples of how one might deal with a few of the most common objections:

"You know, it's funny. Some people look at the six months I took off last year as a big question mark, but that was actually a time when I gained some of the most valuable experience of my professional life. Instead of focusing on normal day-to-day issues, I was able to use that time to develop my skills with _____ and _____. Now I'm able to do _____, which will help me contribute to your team in the following ways…"

"Someone was asking me how the fact that I've only worked for small companies in the past might affect my ability to perform in a larger environment. When I was at X Company I had the privilege of working for someone who came from a Fortune 500 environment. Even though our company was small we incorporated many of the best practices he learned in the larger organizations. It was great for me because I was able to get the best of both worlds."

"I can see how the fact that my compensation used to be much higher could be perceived as a potential problem for my motivation. The truth is I'm far more motivated by the opportunity to take on new challenges and grow as a professional than I am by money. It also turns out that I'm in the fortunate position of being able to live very comfortably on a moderate salary, so I don't have to worry about matching my past income."

"Some employers look at the fact that I've had half a dozen jobs over the past ten years as a negative. They see that much change and assume I'm going to pick up and leave the next time a great opportunity presents itself. To be fair, that was true for most of the past ten years. Recently I've realized/experienced/learned _____, and my biggest goal is to find a home where I can apply the skills gained at all of my past employers in a long-term and meaningful way. This seems like the kind of place where I'd like for that to happen."

More important than the specific content of any of these dialogues is the approach and methodology used in formulating them. The idea is to identify the objection that is most likely to be on the mind of your interviewer, acknowledge it, and address it in a friendly, direct, and conversational way.

FAST TRACK CHALLENGE:

Looking at your resume and background, identify the three objections you are most likely to face in the interview process. When you're done, create a brief dialogue for each that will empower you to proactively mitigate the issue. Follow the format identified above: identify, acknowledge, and address. Once you have a dialogue created, practice saying it out loud a few times, ideally in front of a mirror. The more comfortable you are with what you say and how you say it, the better it will come out in a live situation.

Objection # 1:

Dialogue:

Objection # 2:

Dialogue:

Objection # 3:

Dialogue:

ADDRESSING WEAKNESSES

"Our strength grows out of our weaknesses."

Ralph Waldo Emerson

Imagine a hiring manager says to you, "So, Mike, one of the keys to success on this project is working with Microsoft Project. I don't see that listed anywhere on your resume. Do you have any experience working with Project?" The honest answer is no. What to do?

Most people will give an answer that goes something like, "No, I'm afraid I don't," and then hope to move on to the next question as quickly as possible. It's an honest answer, but also a missed opportunity. Instead of simply saying no and moving on, it could have been an opportunity to transform a weakness and present it as a strength.

Faced with a question to which the answer is "no," such as the one above, an expert interviewer will respond with an intelligent counter. They might say something to the effect of, "you know, I haven't worked with Microsoft

Project, but I do have a great deal of experience with a similar product called Primavera. One thing that really excites me about this position is that it would give me a chance to leverage my strength in project management software while gaining experience with a new tool."

Instead of looking like a person who lacks an important skill set, you have the opportunity to come across as someone with relevant experience and something to gain. Sometimes this will be received more positively than having the exact desired experience and give you a leg up on the competition. Other times it still won't be good enough and you still won't get the job. Either way the perception of you as a resource is likely to be far better than if you simply said "no."

FAST TRACK CHALLENGE:

Take ten minutes to identify one or two weaknesses in your background. Create a brief dialogue for each that empowers you to address the lack of skill or experience in this area in a way that instead focuses on one of your strengths.

WHEN THINGS GET AWKWARD

Everything is going great in your interview, you're nailing the questions, and all of a sudden the conversation takes a serious left turn. The interviewer brings up age, sex, money, or some other weird and awkward topic. What now?

Well, this is really pretty simple. Unless you're in show business, the only one of these you should have to deal with is money. If sex comes up, run for the hills. There's a major problem (and likely lawsuit) just around the corner, so get out as quickly and gracefully as you can.

Age is pretty obvious in an in-person interview and in most places the topic is illegal to discuss explicitly, so it doesn't usually come up in a professional environment. If it does it will usually be approached indirectly (e.g. - "In what year did you complete your degree?"). When that happens, your best bet is to give a direct and confident answer that allows you to move on to the next topic.

Strange and unusual questions sometimes surface in the interview process. It may not happen to you, but then again, maybe it will. If it does, the fastest and most effective way past the awkwardness is to take a breath, restate what you heard, ask for confirmation, and then give a concise, structured answer in the manner highlighted earlier. The process might look something like this:

1) "You'd like to know whether or not I enjoy playing with dolls. Is that correct?"

2) "You know, I did when I was younger but it's been a long time since I busted out the old Barbie collection. How about you?"

OR

2) "You know, I never did when I was a kid, but now I have a young daughter and we have an absolute blast playing with dolls together. Thanks for asking."

The interviewer might be serious about the question, or they might be testing you. If you get weird or defensive, you risk shooting yourself in the foot or raising concerns that are entirely unrelated to the original topic. Questions about your personality or integrity are far more likely to bounce you out of the interview process than your affinity towards dolls (or lack thereof). At decision time the issue in question will either be a factor in the mind of your audience or it won't, and your best bet is handling the topic directly and courteously.

FINISHING STRONG

"Successful people start fast and finish strong."

Bud Bilanich

Performing well through the first ninety percent of the interview doesn't do you a whole lot of good if you blow it at the end or walk away without a legitimate shot at moving forward. Ending on the right note can be tricky, but a couple of proven techniques for making sure you end the interview on a positive note and set yourself up for the next stage of the process are: 1) address any lingering concerns; 2) reinforce your value as a resource; 3) express interest in the opportunity; 4) finish with a handshake and a smile; and 5) follow up with a thank-you letter or email.

ADDRESS LINGERING CONCERNS

When you walk out the door from an interview and the interviewer still has a concern about you or your ability to get the job done, you probably aren't going to get hired. By the time you find out there was an issue the position is likely to have gone to a candidate in whom they feel more confident.

The best time to address issues is when you are "live" with the person who has the concern—face to face if you're on site or by phone if it happens to be a phone interview. Instead of waiting passively for good news and hoping you got things right, consider using one of these phrases to give yourself a shot at gracefully addressing concerns before they rule you out of the opportunity:

"Do you have any other questions about my background or concerns about my ability to bring value to your team?"

"Are there any questions I didn't answer effectively, or on which you'd like further clarification?"

"Is there anything you can see that would prevent me from being the right person for this opportunity?"

If anything shows up at this point, address it with the approach discussed in the overcoming objections section. Acknowledge the validity of the concern and then share in a direct, pleasant way exactly why it shouldn't be an issue or how you can mitigate that concern.

REINFORCE YOUR VALUE AS A RESOURCE

After you address any last concerns, take a moment to review the highlights from earlier parts of the interview, focusing specifically on experiences and qualifications that demonstrate your ability to bring value to their organization. To the best of your ability, leave them with a positive association about you and your ability to contribute to their success.

"You know, I was really happy to hear you're planning to approach this project with method Q. Your model is almost exactly the same as the one we used on my last assignment, and the results were outstanding."

"I'm really glad you're planning to use X. The work we did with that on my last project was some of the most engaging and rewarding of my career. I'm looking forward to the opportunity to applying what I learned in a new environment."

The more effectively you return the focus to what they want and how you can help them get it, the more likely they are to remember and focus on the positive after you leave the interview.

EXPRESS INTEREST

Everyone loves to feel validated, and this is as true for hiring managers and interviewers as it is for individual job seekers. If you like what you've seen in an interview, don't be afraid to let the person know. Odds are, they aren't a mind reader, and hoping they'll "figure it out" isn't a great strategy. Make it clear, but without sounding like a suck-up or coming off as desperate. Here are a couple phrases you can try out at the end of your next interview:

"This sounds like a good opportunity, and I'm very interested in the possibility of continuing our discussion. What should I expect as the next steps?"

"You know, this sounds like a really solid match for my skills and experience. What do you need from me to move things to the next level?"

If these don't feel quite right, come up with a question or two of your own. You don't have to be head over heels to express interest, and wanting to move to the next level isn't the same as a binding commitment. The goal is to put yourself in the driver's seat, and getting to the next phase of the hiring process is part of what it takes to get there.

FINISH WITH A HANDSHAKE AND A SMILE

Finish confident, strong, and appreciative, just like you started. Walk out the door with a big smile, firm handshake, and words of appreciation directed at your interviewer. Let the other person know you appreciate their time and attention, and that you feel confident in your ability to move forward. You can say it any way that feels comfortable to you, but here are a few simple ideas...

"Thanks again for meeting with me today. I really enjoyed our conversation and am looking forward to the possibility of moving things to the next level."

"Thank you again. I really appreciate you spending time with me today and am looking forward to whatever the next steps might be."

Leave on as positive a note as possible. Make the person feel good about meeting with you, let them know you're interested, and show confident optimism about what's going to happen next. If you come from the assumption that there will be a next step, there's a good chance there actually will.

FOLLOW UP WITH A THANK-YOU EMAIL (OR LETTER)

Following an interview with a thank-you email or letter is a simple and impactful way to differentiate yourself from the competition. Most people don't follow up at all, let alone express thanks or appreciation for the time the interviewer(s) invested with them. A thank-you letter isn't just a great practice for making yourself look good. In many cases it's a key criteria for selecting a final candidate.

According to a survey conducted by Careerbuilder.com, lack of a thank-you letter is a criteria used by many managers to SCREEN OUT applicants[8]. In other words, not only does writing a thank-you letter help you stand out in a positive way, it can keep you from being eliminated from the hiring process altogether. The letter doesn't have to be fancy or complicated to be effective. It can be as simple as a quick note to the effect of:

> *Dear _____,*
>
> *Thank you again for taking the time to meet with me yesterday. I really enjoyed interviewing with you and your team and am looking forward to the opportunity to work with you.*
>
> *Best regards,*
>
> *Mike*

OR

> *Hi _____,*
>
> *It was great meeting with you and your team. I really appreciate the time and energy you put into the interview process and deeply enjoyed our conversation. I look forward to hearing from you soon and exploring the possibility of working together.*
>
> *Best regards,*
>
> *Mike*

If you like, you can get more specific and use the letter as an opportunity to reinforce the value you can bring to the organization.

> *Dear _____,*
>
> *It was a pleasure meeting you earlier this week, and I wanted to express my appreciation for the opportunity to interview with your team. After*

---

8   http://www.sys-con.com/node/119856

fifteen years of leading and managing IT healthcare project teams, I believe the opportunity is a great match and that I can bring great value to you and your organization. Please don't hesitate to contact me with any additional questions. I hope we'll be working together in the near future.

Best regards,

Mike

Hi _____,

It was great meeting with you and your team, and I really appreciate the time and energy you spent with me. It was clear that you excel at what you do and push your people to do the same. As an expert IT Healthcare Project Manager I understand the energy that goes into building a team of that caliber, and would love the opportunity to contribute to the effort. Please let me know the next steps, and I'll look forward to being in touch again soon.

Best regards,

Mike

You get the idea. A thank-you letter can be as simple or detailed as you like. You can take the letter to a whole different level by including letters of recommendation and/or work samples as attachments to your thank you email:

Dear _____,

Thanks again for a great meeting yesterday. Interviewing with you and your team made it clear that _____ is a company I'd love to work for. Please don't hesitate to contact me with any further questions. I look forward to moving through the next steps of your hiring process and joining your team.

Best regards,

Mike

P.S. Attached you will find two letters of recommendation and a copy of the project plan we discussed in our meeting. Please let me know if there's anything else I can do to help move the process forward.

Even in an interview that didn't go particularly well it's a great practice to send a thank-you email. You never know when a simple gesture will be the difference in getting a second chance to interview, or who the interviewer might be willing or able to introduce you to. Setting yourself apart as someone with great manners and follow up is a good idea all the time. In the case of a "bad" interview, the letter may be something very simple, like:

Dear _____,

Thank you again for the opportunity to interview for the role with your team. I appreciate your time and look forward to staying in touch. If there's anything I can do to be of service, please don't hesitate to let me know.

Best regards,

Mike

People frequently leave interviews saying to themselves, "Wow, that went poorly," only to get a call a few days later requesting a second interview. Rather than make assumptions, make a conscious habit of sending thank-you letters. Even if that specific person doesn't hire you, you'll have left a positive impression on someone who may have the power to help you at some other point in your career.

FAST TRACK CHALLENGE:

Draft a thank-you letter template that can be customized and sent out immediately after your next interview. Save this letter in a place where it can be easily accessed and modified for future use.

SALARY NEGOTIATION

"The minute you settle for less than you deserve, you get even less than you settled for."

Maureen Dowd

✥ ✥ ✥

I met Noy while recruiting consultants for a niche financial services firm in the southern California market. The company was a top-notch organization with a project that required consultants with a very specific technical expertise. Noy's resume was a direct match and he had the presentation skills and work samples to back it up, so immediately after concluding the initial screening process we set the interview wheel in motion.

Noy had a phone screen with our client later that same week and landed an offer to join their team after a single in-person meeting ten days later. He started work the following Monday along with a team of four other consultants.

Although he was less experienced than his peers, Noy outlasted the other consultants hired for the same project and received generally positive reviews from his manager. As he wrapped up his first engagement for us, we set about finding him a second. Within a few weeks and a handful of interviews, we placed him into a full-time position with a Fortune 500 company.

Shortly after signing the employment papers, Noy came back to us with news of a late offer from another employer. The other job paid better than the role he had accepted, but he promised to honor his acceptance if our client matched the offer. We went back to the hiring manager, shared the situation, and requested a salary increase to match the other offer. She passed the request along to HR and promised to respond within a day or two.

In the meantime, Noy went back to the other employer and let them know he was expecting a counteroffer. He told them that they would need to up the ante to keep him interested in the position. They did, coming through with an offer significantly higher than the first. Elated, Noy decided to see just how far he could take the game of one-upmanship.

A day later our client came through with approval for the requested salary hike. Instead of accepting these terms and starting the job as promised, Noy told us about the increased offer from the other employer and threatened to renege on his acceptance if we didn't meet the same target. We told him he needed to honor his commitment and start the new position as promised.

Unhappy with our response, Noy called the hiring manager directly. He explained that the other company had increased their offer. Even so, he would still be happy to accept the position on her team if she would simply commit to an extra ten thousand dollars per year.

The manager had already gone out on a limb to get the first increase and didn't like this turn of events at all. She realized very quickly that she'd been pulled into a bidding war and didn't want any part of it. She also decided that she wanted someone on her team that could be counted on to keep their word and honor their commitments. A short while after hanging up with Noy she called us to withdraw the offer and start a new search for the right candidate.

Unfortunately for Noy the story doesn't end there. It turned out that the managers were friends from a shared industry association and talked to each other regularly. The next time they spoke it came out that they'd both been trying to hire the same person and talked about what had happened in that process. When the other manager realized that Noy had initiated the bidding war *after* committing to another position, he decided to withdraw his offer as well. That left Noy with zero offers, two burned bridges, and a tough job market to tackle.

The rollercoaster didn't stop there, either. Our team had a solid track record with Noy and after receiving a number of heartfelt apologies, we offered guidance on how to handle things better in the future and committed to helping him find his next project.

After a few months of searching, we identified an extraordinary opportunity with a privately held financial services firm with hundreds of billions in assets under management. It was a contract-to-hire role and the work was cutting-edge, so there were great opportunities for salary and career growth. We put Noy into the interview process, and true to form, he landed an offer.

This time he wisely accepted the position without hesitation and jumped into the project full force. As was the case in his first project for us, initial reports from the hiring manager indicated that he was doing great work. Our choice to give Noy another chance seemed thoroughly vindicated.

Five and a half months later we got a call from Human Resources letting us know that Noy was being released from his contract ahead of schedule. I was shocked. We'd just spent weeks in discussions with HR about transitioning him from his contract role into a full time position, and less than three days earlier the manager had assured us that Noy was on track for a relatively speedy conversion.

The last step was a simple approval from corporate and Noy's long term professional future would be secured. The process could take as little as two weeks or as long as two months. No big deal either way. All he had to do was keep his head down and focus on delivering high-quality work.

He couldn't do it. The stress and impatience got to him, and Noy decided to try his hand at speeding things up a bit.

Ignoring the fact that the hiring process had already been initiated, and ignoring our guidance to stay focused on delivering results, he went to his manager and explained that he had received a full-time offer from another employer. The position was with a competitor, he said, and they had given him exactly one week to make a decision. For that reason, he explained, his boss needed to accelerate the hiring process or he would have no choice but resign and take the other position.

Instead of pushing for the offer to come out faster, Noy's manager said, "Congratulations. That sounds like a great opportunity. You should take it." He walked down the hall to HR and ended the contract right then and there.

There wasn't another offer, and this time Noy was out of work for the better part of four months. Ouch!

WHAT'S THE BIG DEAL?

Negotiation is one of the most important—and trickiest—aspects of the job search process. It has a profound impact on income and professional growth, yet very few people have any particular skill or training on the topic. The rewards of effective negotiation are significant, and the consequences of a serious blunder can be quite far-reaching (especially in the context of career).

The fear of negotiation in general, and salary negotiation in specific, is shared by most of humanity. As professionals, we're afraid of messing up and losing opportunities and equally afraid of settling for lower offers than could have been landed if a better job was done in the negotiation process.

Unfortunately, these fears are completely valid. Job seekers routinely mess up negotiations and get themselves rejected by potential employers. They lose opportunities, accept unnecessarily low offers, and miss out on chances to positively impact their career trajectory. These things happen each and every day.

Aside from the obvious and practical reasons to be concerned about negotiation, an underlying cause for this fear may be the way we collectively define the process itself. According to the North American version of the Encarta Dictionary, the word negotiation relates to the "resolving of disagreements" and means "the reaching of agreement through discussion and compromise.[9]"

Disagreement, discussion, and compromise. No wonder most people dread negotiation...it sounds like a pretty awful way to start a new employment experience.

Clearly negotiation has a place in the world—it can be fun at a garage sale or an overseas market—but does the traditional paradigm work in the context of employment? Can you grind a future employer or employee over money and come to a genuinely productive resolution? Does the paradigm

---

9   www.dictionary.com

of one person winning and the other losing actually serve either party in the long run?

Traditional negotiation works in the context of one-time events and transaction. You can negotiate the price on a car, cell phone plan, or garage sale item, pay or get on a payment plan, and be done. You never have to interact with the other person again if you don't want to, and your contact with the company or service provider is limited to brief interactions of your choosing.

Employment, however, is not a one-time transaction. It's an ongoing series of interactions and interpersonal relationships. Salary negotiation is simply one interaction among many. After it's done you have to live and work with the people on the other side of the equation for the foreseeable future. If one person walks away feeling like they've lost or been forced to compromise it sets up a disempowering context for the rest of the relationship. When it comes to employment, the paradigm of someone winning and the other person losing doesn't serve either party in the long run.

THE ART OF WORKPLACE NEGOTIATION

In the world of hiring, firing, and day-to-day employment, negotiation isn't about negotiating at all — at least in the traditional sense of the word. It's about making EVERYONE feel like a winner, and that means minimizing or eliminating the concept of "negotiation" altogether.

A win-win hiring process ends with a motivated and enthusiastic employee on one side, and an employer who feels good about writing their paycheck on the other.

When an employee receives inadequate compensation they're unlikely to stay long or contribute to the best of their ability. When an employer overpays on salary and can't get a positive return on investment, they have no choice but look for a lower-cost resource. Both situations represent a two sided loss. A salary negotiation is win-win when everyone feels good about the value they're giving and receiving.

As the employee, your job at this stage of the game is to identify the highest starting salary at which everyone will feel like they've gotten a great deal. You feel happy because you're receiving a rewarding level of compensation, and they feel great because they hired an outstanding employee who can reasonably be expected to deliver a positive return on investment.

A "just one winner" approach is fine in sports and perhaps tolerable in one-time transactions, but it is a very bad strategy for anything longer. When it comes to career, business partnerships, and long term relationships, win-win is much, much better.

CREATING WIN-WIN

"Adopt a new philosophy of cooperation in which everybody wins."

W. Edwards Deming

By now most of the work required to carry the hiring process through to a successful conclusion has already been done. You've made it easy to recognize your value by writing a great resume, identifying the goals of your audience, and demonstrating the capacity to make a positive contribution. They have a business need and the motivation required to make a hiring commitment. It's a situation in which everyone is set up to win.

The next step is to come to agreement on a compensation package that matches your salary requirements with the perceived value you bring to the table. Sometimes this happens on the first shot and no negotiation is required. Sometimes it takes a little more work to come to productive resolution. In either case, it's a good idea to go into the final stage of the hiring process with goals that are aligned with market rates and expectations, along with the know-how required to close the gap if one exists.

SETTING ATTAINABLE GOALS

There's a delicate balance between the value you can bring to an employer and the amount of money they're likely to pay in order to receive that value.

The reward to the employer has to be equal to or greater than the cost of hiring you as a resource, and the reward to you must be equal to or greater than that which you can receive elsewhere on the market. If either condition isn't met, the terms don't make sense and the situation is untenable.

Part of having an attainable salary goal means coming to terms with what the other party will consider a fair and legitimate offer. Some companies have clearly defined pay grades (in which case there's not a lot to negotiate over) and others don't. In both cases they are likely to deliver an offer that falls within accepted industry standards and recognized compensation "norms." Expecting otherwise will set you up to feel disappointment, even if a genuinely outstanding offer is extended. Regardless of the outcome, that's a pretty lousy state of affairs.

The variety of potential circumstances in which you might find yourself as a job seeker is nearly infinite, so it would be senseless to try and address every possible scenario. For that reason this section simplifies the equation down to two basic variables—employed and unemployed—along with general guidelines on what to expect in each situation. You can use your own judgment to modify these guidelines to fit the unique circumstances of your industry, profession, and life situation.

As you read, please note that the numbers presented are in relation to current compensation (if you're working), most recent compensation (if you're not), or the approximate average of your last several packages (if there's recently been a dramatic change in your income). Standardized salaries and pay rates do exist in some companies, but expecting a given job to come at a fixed compensation level isn't realistic. Work experience and interview performance are likely to weigh into the equation as well, but salary history is almost always a determining factor.

For better or worse, past compensation is a measuring stick used by most employers to determine how much money to offer a potential employee. The words "I was underpaid" don't constitute a valid argument for a major salary increase. Not in the mind of an employer, anyway.

Employed:

If you're working at a great job and have a highly desirable skill set, you're in the ideal position for pulling in a healthy salary increase. Typical increases for the gainfully employed range from five to fifteen percent, with five percent being about normal, ten percent being really good, and fifteen percent or more falling into the realm of outstanding.

An increase in the seven to ten percent range is generally a viable target for the gainfully employed. It's a big enough increase to make a bottom line difference, but not so big that you're likely to raise red flags with a potential employer. If both parties are positioned to get value from the relationship, you've got a great shot at landing the salary you want.

Asking for a significantly larger increase, even while employed, can raise eyebrows and potentially get you bounced out of the hiring process. This is especially likely in an employment market with a great deal of available talent and a high degree of competition for type of job you're seeking. As a potential employee, you have to weigh the value of landing a higher salary against the risk of losing the position altogether. If you really want the job, balance your expectations against what the other party will consider reasonable.

It's worth noting that there are a number of completely valid reasons for going after a larger-than-ordinary pay increase. Getting actively recruited out of your current position for a role with a competitor provides a legitimate justification for going after a sizable jump in pay. You have specific domain expertise and a lot to lose if things don't work out, and there should be at least as much to gain in order to make it worth your while to take the risk.

Other commonly accepted reasons for a healthy boost include completing a degree or certification program, possessing an unusually hard-to-find skill set, or preemptively demonstrating the ability to deliver a bottom line contribution. There are undoubtedly other circumstances that are equally viable, so use your own best judgment to analyze your personal situation and set a salary target. Pick a number that is attainable, likely to make you happy, and unlikely to scare off a great offer.

Unemployed:

If you're unemployed, things are a little different. Instead of aiming for a modest or aggressive increase, you may have to accept that break even is a positive outcome and a small step backwards is highly probable. When you're out of work an increase is relatively unlikely, much less a sizable boost in pay. Being unemployed is a competitive disadvantage, and with very few exceptions (such as completing an MBA or coming back from service in the armed forces), it is far easier to secure an increase in pay when you're already employed than otherwise. It just is.

Landing an increase isn't impossible when you're out of work. It can be done. It just shouldn't be an expectation. Anything that falls within a reasonable distance from your most recent salary should be considered a fair and viable offer. Even if an offer is noticeably lower than your most recent pay you should seriously consider saying yes—especially if the rest of the details are good.

If you happen to be unemployed in a recession or depressed hiring market there's a very real chance of stepping back quite a bit before you're in a position to move forward again. A down market means increased competition and decreased salaries. It's not the right time to hold out for a "perfect" position or stubbornly wait for someone to pay what you're accustomed to earning. Employment is power, and once you're employed (even at a lower pay grade), the pendulum swings back in your direction.

Besides, sometimes taking a step backwards can open doors and provide opportunities for growth that can't be seen or imagined from your current vantage point. If you're unemployed, get back to work as quickly as you can at the best salary you can, and make your next move from there.

CLOSING A SALARY GAP

"Price is what you pay. Value is what you get."

Warren Buffett

Let's say you're working right now at a position that pays $65,000 per year plus benefits. You're in the final stages of negotiating for an exciting opportunity with an employer to whom you can provide great value. The overall benefits are comparable, and you believe your skills, experience, and talent justify at least a ten percent increase. Your heart is set on a minimum salary of $71,500 per year. That's what you want, and that's what it's going to take to have you show up for work excited about making a difference.

When the offer comes in, the number is actually $68,250—a respectable five percent increase and in line with market pay. Not bad, but it doesn't meet your goal and it doesn't have you jumping out of your chair to resign from your current position. What next? Is it time to play hard ball? Do you capitulate and take the lower offer? What's the right thing to do?

Actually, before doing anything you should step back, take a deep breath, and look at the good news. They want to hire you. You want to go to work for them. They want a motivated and enthusiastic employee. You want to go to the office feeling excited about your career and happy with your finances. Your expectations are optimistic but reasonable, and they've started negotiations at a respectable level. Interests are aligned on all fronts, and that means everyone is very close to getting what they want.

So how do you get from where you are to the offer you really want? Better yet, how do you bring home the offer you want and build even more good will in the process? That's creating an ideal situation, and that's where a value proposition comes into play.

A value proposition is a proposal that demonstrates why choosing in favor of a given request makes sense from a business perspective. Creating a value proposition assists the other person in answering the all-important question, "What's in it for me?" It says, "Here are the benefits to YOU of giving me what I want," and in many situations a well-delivered value proposition will help a job seeker close the gap between an initial offer and a target salary.

The major difference between a value proposition and a traditional negotiation is the focus of the conversation. A negotiation is about coercing the other person to give you what you want. A value proposition focuses on what THEY want and how you can help them get it. The difference is subtle but significant. A compelling value proposition is one that makes sound business sense and offers a pathway to everyone achieving their goals. That's the key.

FAST TRACK CHALLENGE:

Answer the following series of questions and put yourself in a position to: 1) identify the maximum level of compensation that can be reasonably justified in your current situation, and 2) help you develop a clear value proposition for a prospective employer.

I am Employed/Unemployed:

My Current/Most Recent Compensation is:

Base Salary_____

    Bonuses_____

    Benefits (approximate monetary value) _____

    Vacation Time_____

    Other_____

    Total_____

Desired Increase:____%

Target Compensation:_____

Which of my skills and experiences are directly applicable to this opportunity?

What tangible results can I commit to producing in exchange for the increase in compensation?

What am I willing do in exchange for the increase in compensation?

Why is this increase in the best interest of the employer?

What are the additional benefits to the employer of giving me what I want?

What will they have to do to secure my complete commitment and focus?

After you finish answering the questions, step back and evaluate your responses from the perspective of a hiring authority. If the roles were reversed, how much impact would this information have on your decision-making process? Put yourself in their shoes and think about which pieces of information would make the biggest difference to you. If you wouldn't find a particular topic compelling, they probably won't either.

DEFINING AND COMMUNICATING A VALUE PROPOSITION

"Talk to people about themselves and they will listen for hours."

Benjamin Disraeli

When you share a value proposition the emphasis is on the benefit to the other party. Always. The intention is to make one thing clear—that it's in their own best interest to agree to your request. Your delivery should be clear, concise, and confident, without coming across as arrogant or cocky. In order to accomplish this goal it's a good idea to use a structure that empowers your message to come through as simply and effectively as possible.

Start by expressing appreciation. Gratitude is extraordinarily powerful and helps set the tone for an amicable and productive discussion. Next, reiterate one of their goals and share how you will help them achieve it. Last, clarify exactly what you are looking for; the other party needs to know exactly what is being proposed or they won't be able to say yes to you.

1) Gratitude; 2) Goals 3) Value; and 4) Requirements

Employed:

The value proposition you present when employed can be relatively simple. Returning to the earlier scenario in which the offer was $68,500 instead of $71,500, one might respond by saying, "Thanks so much for this offer and your interest in hiring me. This position seems like a great match, and I'm confident my experience with X and Y will help you achieve Z. $68,500 is a fair offer, but I have my heart set on a salary of at least $71,500. If we can meet at that level you have my word that I'll accept the position and come in 100 percent focused, committed, and happy. Can you make that happen?"

You've expressed appreciation, focused on their goals, and made the terms of your proposal exceedingly clear. The number you've requested isn't so high that you'll raise red flags or create impossible expectations, but it's high enough that they'll respect your self-confidence. By accepting your proposal, they get a focused and committed employee who will help them achieve their goals.

If the work can realistically be valued at $71,500 or more, you've got a very strong chance of hitting your target. They get what they want, and you get what you want. Everyone wins.

If they can't (or won't) meet your expectations, they'll either make a counter-proposal to meet in the middle or leave the offer "as is." At that point you have to decide whether or not the move is justified. If you can be happy with the offer they've extended (which represents a fair and reasonable pay increase), accept the job and start the new position with enthusiasm and appreciation. If not, decline the offer with gratitude and stay where you are until the right opportunity comes along.

Unemployed:

When you're out of a job it often makes sense to accept the first reasonable offer that comes your way—especially if there are other qualified applicants competing for the same position. Your best bet is to say yes immediately and get back to work as quickly as you can. Even if the salary and opportunity aren't ideal, you'll be in a better situation than your unemployed counterparts and can make your next move from a position of strength rather than weakness.

If you think you can do better or the offer is too low to accept, do your best to create a value proposition that makes a win-win possible. Given that you're not negotiating from the same position of strength, your proposal may need to include a more quantifiable benefit to make sense in the mind of the employer.

In this case you might say something like, "Thank you very much for the offer and your interest in hiring me. I'm really excited about the possibility of coming to work for you and am confident my experience with X and Y will help you achieve Z. That said, I'm looking for a minimum base salary of $65,000. If you can meet me at that level I'll commit to not only making sure we achieve the goals discussed in the interview process, but also to contributing (extra hours, accomplishments, etc). Can we make that work?"

As before, this structure provides a reasonable possibility of getting what you want. You've expressed appreciation, reinforced your value to the company, and made a commitment to something that is meaningful in their world (your time, an outcome, etc). At this point, your best bet is to sit quiet and let them decide if what you've proposed makes sense. If it does, great. You'll have landed a better salary and can go to work happy. If not, decide whether or not the value you'll receive from being employed makes it worthwhile to say yes to the original offer. Unless you have other viable prospects in queue, it probably does.

Got Nothing?

If you can't create a value proposition that demonstrates more value to your employer than the opportunity provides in return, you're probably getting the better end of the deal. You've either been offered a strong starting salary or will be stepping into a position that allows you to learn and grow.

A great salary is fantastic, and the opportunity to develop or strengthen your skill set is a completely legitimate form of compensation in its own right. Skills and experience equal market value, and that means the next time you interview for an opportunity you will be able to create a compelling case for a better salary or bigger perks. That's a good thing. In either case, you should probably consider accepting the offer "as is."

FAST TRACK CHALLENGE:

Create one clearly defined value proposition following the format outlined above. When you're done, practice delivering your proposal in front of a mirror or video camera until your presentation is sharp and compelling. You should be able to look yourself in the eye and know that if the situation were reversed, you'd say yes to someone presenting the exact same case to you.

1) Express gratitude; 2) Reiterate their goals 3) Reinforce your value; and 4) Clarify what it will take to receive that value.

AVOIDING THE DEAL KILLERS

"Learn from the mistakes of others. You can't live long enough to make them all yourself."

Eleanor Roosevelt

Noy learned the hard way that there are a lot of places where salary and employment discussions can go sideways. In a matter of just a few negotiations he covered almost all of the most common deal killers. He bluffed, threatened, instigated a bidding war, circumvented the proper chain of communication, delivered an ultimatum (twice), blatantly misrepresented his situation, and reneged on the terms of an agreement. These bloopers cost him several great opportunities, tens of thousands of dollars in income, and a number of high-profile relationships.

The negotiation process (and life in general) can be dynamic. Simplifying the equation minimizes the number of opportunities for things to go sideways and maximizes the odds of reaching a mutually beneficial arrangement. That's why it's so useful to set realistic goals and use value propositions to communicate them in a customer focused way.

It's equally useful to learn from the mistakes of others. Rather than bluff or threaten, create situations and circumstances where you actually HAVE leverage. If you want to play hard ball, bring you're A-game and suit up. That means having a backup offer on the table when you go to make a power play. It means having the full facts and details about why you deserve a raise or promotion, supporting documentation to validate your claims, and the chops to walk away if you don't get what you want.

Instead of getting into a bidding war, weigh the merits of the various offers as they come in and use value propositions to push them higher. The specific numbers you propose don't need to be the same with every employer. Each opportunity is different. One may have a better location while the other offers a larger opportunity for growth, a better manager, or a better benefits package. Be intelligent and make the best decisions you can.

If you come to a place where you feel stuck, ask for advice from a coach or mentor. Recognizing pitfalls is one thing, but successfully navigating them is another. Working with someone who has successfully done what you're hoping to do can help you work your way through a potentially sticky situation and come out a winner.

SUMMARY

Your best shot at maximizing job offers is to minimize traditional win-lose dynamics and instead use value propositions to create outcomes that work for everyone. Your goal is to push the compensation envelope as far as possible and still be in a position to deliver enough value to justify every penny. Here's a quick recap of the highlights from this section:

1. Set clear and realistic expectations for yourself about the level of compensation your prospective employer is likely to pay based on your past compensation and recognized industry "norms."
2. Define and communicate value propositions that make it easy for a prospective employer to say yes.
3. Avoid playing games and falling victim to common negotiation blunders.
4. Ask for help and guidance from a coach or mentor any time you feel stuck (when in doubt, reach out).

YES OR NO...CLOSING WITH CLASS

"The art of leadership is the art of saying no, not yes. It is very easy to say yes."

Tony Blair

☙❧

By the time an offer gets extended, there's been an investment of time and energy by both parties. The employer has invested their resources into the process of evaluating you, and you've invested your time and talent into making it through the evaluation process. You wrote a resume that caught their attention, brought value to the interview process, and carried yourself well enough that they think you can contribute to their team. Now what?

Now you have to make a decision about whether or not the offer is right, and communicate that decision to the relevant stakeholders. Whether or not you choose to accept a given opportunity, it's important to leave the other party feeling appreciated and respected. This is especially true if they end up on the losing side of the equation. There's an art to saying yes, and perhaps an even greater art to saying no.

In either case, the secret to effectively responding to job offers is to: 1) Be Decisive, 2) Be Appreciative, and 3) Be of Service.

BE DECISIVE

Nobody enjoys feeling like a second choice. Even worse is to be a second choice who is left hanging while the other party is out shopping for better offers. When it comes time to accept or decline an offer, the best approach is a clear and decisive response—either affirmative or negative. Waffling back and forth makes you look weak, and stalling for more time while waiting for a better deal leaves a bad taste in everyone's mouth.

Obviously you need to seriously consider and weigh the merits of your different career options – that's a given – but the best time to do so is before an offer is extended and you're on the hook to deliver a decision.

Although most people will "understand" if you want to be thorough and think about your options, everyone would much rather you be excited and enthusiastic about joining their team (or clear about why you aren't). They want a happy and enthusiastic "yes" or solid and decisive "no"—not a wimpy "let me get back to you later." They want to move forward, and for that to happen you need to give a clear and decisive answer. That's why it's best to avoid phrases like:

"Let me think about it."

"I have a few other offers to consider."

"Let me go home and talk to my (husband, wife, partner, significant other, etc)."

Sometimes you may really need more time (like when you have to sort your way through multiple offers), but to the greatest extent possible, do your strategizing and thinking in advance. Walk through the various likely scenarios by yourself and your significant other BEFORE they come up in the real world. Look at what you will do if an offer comes in lower than hoped for, on target, or high. Think about what you'll do if multiple companies make viable offers, and how you will respond to each possibility.

Get "buy in" or agreement from your significant other (if necessary and relevant) before you're in the actual situation with a prospective employer and get asked to make a decision. Create parameters for Yes, No, and Maybe. Empower yourself to make a decision on the spot or instantly deliver a counter-proposal, and to do either with confidence and enthusiasm. If you're going to take time to think, proactively set a deadline for coming to a decision and communicate it clearly with everyone involved. As you respond to those making the offers, consider using phrases like:

"Yes, absolutely. I'm really looking forward to being part of your team and can't wait to get started."

"Awesome! You'll have the paperwork back to you by tomorrow morning, and I'll look forward to starting in two weeks."

"No, thank you. I really appreciate the offer, but based on everything I see, a move doesn't make sense at this time."

"No, thank you. I've chosen to accept another position, but really appreciate your interest in hiring me. I hope our paths cross again in the future!"

"Thank you very much. The position sounds great and the offer is really close to my target number. If we can meet at X, you have my commitment to be on board and ready to hit the ground running two weeks from today."

"Thanks so much for the offer. It's a really interesting position, and I'm certain my experience with Z will help bring your project home successfully. If you can increase the starting salary to X, I'll give my notice immediately and be ready to start in two weeks."

"Thank you so much for the offer. Next Friday is my deadline for making a final decision, and I'll be in touch with my answer no later than noon."

Prepare to respond confidently and decisively or deliver a value proposition that outlines new terms and conditions that would be acceptable to you. Even if you do end up needing a day or two to consider your options, thinking through the various possibilities in advance will be excellent preparation for making an intelligent decision. The people you interact with will respect you more, and that's valuable no matter what choice you make. Equally valuable is to...

BE APPRECIATIVE

Over the course of the interview process you've become a person to those on the other side of the hiring equation. You're not just a skill set or a means to an end. Not anymore. The people you've interacted with are quite literally invested in your success. They think you can make a positive contribution and they want you on their team, usually for both personal and professional reasons. They have "picked you," and that's a great honor.

Regardless of whether or not you return the favor by accepting their offer, it's good form to show these people that you respect and appreciate them as well—both as professionals and as human beings. Let them know you value the time and energy they have invested, that you appreciate their confidence in you, and that you want to help them succeed in the achievement of their goals. Say thank you, and then demonstrate your gratitude with real world action.

BE OF SERVICE

When you accept an offer and start a new job, there is ample opportunity to provide value and be of service. You'll get a chance to contribute every day, five days a week or more, for the foreseeable future.

When you decline an offer, however, there is a very limited period of time in which you can do something of significant value and impact. Taking the initiative to be helpful in the midst of turning down a job offer can make a world of difference to the people you've connected with. The effort doesn't have to be extraordinary to be impactful. To the contrary, even a simple gesture can set you apart in their minds for a very long time.

The next time you say no to an opportunity, follow up by putting them in touch with someone who would be a good match for the position. Offer a suggestion on how they might be able to entice the right candidate to join their team. Share a tip on where people with a similar skill set might be found and how to make contact with them.

Do something to be useful, regardless of how big or small. As much as anything else, the folks you're dealing with will remember your willingness to be helpful at a time when most others aren't. That's the kind of move that pays long-term dividends.

FAST TRACK CHALLENGE:

On your own or with your significant other, create parameters for accepting or declining the next job offer that comes your way. Define what it will take to elicit an immediate yes, decisive no, or tactfully delivered value proposition.

QUITTING WITH CLASS

"Take this job and shove it."

Johnny Paycheck

Once you've committed to a new opportunity there's always the dreaded next step—tendering your resignation. Mr. Paycheck's song may summarize your sentiments to a T, but even if you're thrilled to get away from your current employer, resigning can be an unpleasant experience. It also creates a brief window of opportunity during which you can set yourself up to leave on better terms than existed during your tenure.

Quitting is almost always stressful, but there are ways to minimize the negativity and maximize your remaining time with the company. The first key is to avoid procrastination, and the second is to take advantage of the final opportunity to make a difference. The latter is covered in the Making a Powerful Transition section just ahead. Procrastination gets dealt with now.

Instead of putting off the inevitable discomfort of resigning, act immediately. Don't wait for the perfect opportunity or moment to give your notice. There isn't one. The more you delay and postpone, the more stressful the process will become. Quitting a job is a lot like pulling off a Band-Aid. A quick tug and the pain is over; a prolonged pull makes it sting a lot longer.

A simple way to break through the fear and inertia is to sit down and write professional but decisive letters of resignation, one to each of your immediate supervisors. Proof read them (several times), run spell check, and then hand them to the relevant people. These letters and the accompanying resignation conversations need to be delivered in person rather than via a phone call, email, or a text message. Although it might feel the same, quitting a job is not the same as a teenage break-up. Protocol dictates that, to the greatest extent possible, it needs to be done in person.

A personalized letter of resignation will force you to crystallize your thoughts, confirm your commitment to the new course of action, and make your intention abundantly clear to the other party. It should include a clear statement of intention, a decisive expression of resolve, a genuine sentiment of appreciation, and an offer of assistance in making the transition as seamless as possible. A sample letter might look something like this:

> *Dear Susan,*
>
> *It is with a combination of sadness and anticipation that I tender my resignation from the role of project manager here at Z Company. Your*

guidance, coaching, and mentorship have meant a great deal to me over the years, and I can't express enough appreciation for all that you've done for me. My time here has been extremely valuable, and I will always appreciate the energy that you put into my personal and professional growth. I am a far better leader and project manager as a result of your help and attention, and I'll always be grateful for the support and guidance you've provided.

That said, my decision to resign is final, and I appreciate you honoring my commitment to move forward with another employer at this point in my career. I will do everything in my power to help you find a suitable replacement prior to my departure in two weeks, and will work with the team to ensure the new resource is brought up to speed as quickly as possible. Thanks again for everything.

All my best,
Mike

Be clear with your language, direct about your intentions, and resolved to follow your chosen course of action. Offer to be of service for the duration of your employment, but don't lead them to believe there is a chance you will change your mind. It's too late for that. Now it is time to move on.

COPING WITH COUNTERS

You've gone through your decision-making process, come to a final conclusion, and delivered a nicely written and clearly decisive letter of resignation. It's over now, right? Actually, no. It isn't. Not always.

What if you turn in your resignation and your boss refuses to accept? What if they won't let you go without a fuss and fight? What happens when, despite your best efforts to say adios, they do everything in their power to keep you around? What happens when they make you a really compelling counteroffer? Now what?

Headhunters are admittedly biased on this topic. A counteroffer simultaneously threatens a client relationship and a commission check, and you can imagine how much anyone likes hearing that kind of news. So yes, we're biased. No question. But we also have a great deal of experience watching what happens over the long haul. Experience tells us that most of the time it's a bad idea to go down that path.

Everything else aside, accepting a counteroffer requires breaking your word and going back on a commitment. Never a good idea. It also means ignoring the reasons you were looking for a new job in the first place (if you were in fact looking), and sets you up for a whole host of trust and credibility issues with your current employer regardless of how your resignation came to be.

Even knowing it's a bad idea to consider a counteroffer, it's easy to get caught up in the flattery and positive vibes they inspire. A counteroffer is like a sweet whisper saying, "We love you," "You're too valuable to lose," and "Yes, we'll be happy to pay you more money to stay and grace us with your presence."

Who wouldn't want to feel that way? It's all love and kisses until you put it in perspective, and perspective tells you there are reasons you were ready to walk out that door. It also tells you that you've already made a commitment to do so.

That's why it's a very good idea to think about what you really want long before walking in the door to turn in your resignation (and probably before accepting the opportunity to interview in the first place). Once you deliver a letter of resignation everything changes. The rules of fair play change, and so do your relationships with management and peers.

Instead of flip-flopping on your word and making an infamously poor career decision, do your thinking and strategizing in advance. If there's a chance of getting what you want without having to quit your job, do everything in your power to make it happen BEFORE turning in your resignation.

Money, environment, and career growth issues are among the most common reasons to resign and later rethink the decision. In many cases these issues can be resolved through dialogue and communication. Try to make things work with your current employer first. After you've exhausted your options, consider making a career change.

MAKING A POWERFUL TRANSITION

Most people experience the time between resigning from one position and starting at a new one as a period of stress and chaos or a momentary respite from the whirlwind of professional responsibilities. For the fast track professional it is neither. In business, as in music, sports, and the martial arts, an effective transition is a precise and measured process. The power of a transition is a key differentiator between master and apprentice, expert and amateur.

For a Fast Tracker, the transition is an integral part of the career growth process. It is either a period of profound and conscious relaxation, or of intense and disciplined action. One approach replenishes energy and focus, while the other sets the stage for an uncommonly rapid and productive ramp-up period. While either approach can be extremely effective, the first is only a viable option if there is a significant gap in time between finishing one job and starting the next.

Profound and conscious relaxation requires the intentional unplugging from ordinary sources of stress and discord. Maximizing the quality of down time demands purposeful and intelligent planning. The goal of following this path is to emerge completely refreshed, rejuvenated, and ready to start a new job with renewed energy, focus, and passion. The conditions required to create this type of rejuvenation are a matter of personal preference and disposition, and you will be left to your own devices to make it happen.

The practice of making powerful transitions is a similarly disciplined and intentional process. It isn't easy and doesn't allow for the momentary respite that deep relaxation makes possible, but it does create a very distinct form of leverage that very few of your counterparts are likely to replicate. The remainder of this section focuses on a handful of techniques used by elite professionals to make a powerful and effective transition.

MAKING A GRACEFUL EXIT

In the rush to get out and get prepared for a new job it's easy to lose sight of the things you need to do make a graceful transition out of the current one. Most people do exactly that, leaving employers scrambling just to stay on level ground. Since you never know when or where you'll run into the folks you've worked with in the past or how they might influence your career trajectory, that's not a particularly good strategy.

Regardless of how happy you are to GET OUT and move on, don't drop the ball. It's never a good idea to burn bridges in the business world (or anywhere else for that matter). If your relationships are on less than solid ground, the transition out is your last real chance to solidify things before you're gone and it's too late. A great exit can change perspectives about who you are as a person and as an employee, and it is well worth the effort to take full advantage of your final opportunity to do this.

Why bother? For one, why not? What could it possibly hurt to go out on the best terms possible, even if it means a little extra work? For another, you're eventually going to run into a situation where past relationships affect your future success. It's going to happen, and when it does, it might as well work in your favor.

Given a choice, what would you rather have someone say about you?

"You know, we didn't always have a great working relationship, but she showed a lot of class when she left the company. Her work got finished, she put in time to interview a replacement, and even helped the new guy get up to speed after starting her other job. Based on all that, I can give a solid recommendation with no problem."

—OR—

"You know, she did a relatively good job while she was working here, but when she quit she left us hanging with a major deadline on the horizon. Our whole project was set back months because we couldn't figure out what she'd been doing and didn't have a competent backup to take over her tasks. If it had ended differently I might recommend her, she did a lot of damage on the way out."

You don't have to have perfect references to get hired—nobody does—but the people you've worked with should have a generally positive outlook about you in general. Your transition out might be the last opportunity you get to turn a thumbs down into a thumbs up, and it's a good idea to do everything in your power to make it happen.

What can you do to help make for a graceful transition? Here are a few suggestions:

- Make a list of EVERYTHING you are currently working on and the specific status of each item. Take the list to your manager and find out which are the most important items to complete before you make a final exit.

- Make a list of all of your day-to-day tasks, roles, and responsibilities accompanied by the tools, technologies, or techniques used in the performance of your duties. In essence you are writing the job description for your replacement, which you are far more qualified to do than anyone else. Since this description is based on the reality of the job rather than an arbitrary wish list, the effort can be an invaluable aid in hiring and training the new person.

- Clear your personal schedule for the month following your resignation. Use this time to help your past employer find, interview, and train a replacement candidate. If necessary, make yourself available to evaluate potential candidates in your off hours – even if it's after you start your next position.

- Volunteer to spend a few evenings or weekends helping the new person get up to speed. The time investment doesn't have to be significant to leave an impression that can last for years.

- Wrap up as much of your work as humanly possible before your last day. This may involve overtime or weekend hours, but you're almost out of there and the extra stress won't last long. It's worth a little pain to close like a champion.

As you review this list you may think of more things you could do to make a positive difference. If time allows, by all means jump in and get them done. Realistically, if you take the initiative on these and follow through on the recommendations for preparing to start your next job, you won't have much time available for additional activities.

When time gets thin, which it probably will, put your energy into the activities that will have the most immediate and obvious benefit to those around you (i.e. those your manager described as most important). Your exit won't be perfect, but do the best you can to make a difference and you'll set yourself miles apart from the average ex-employee. Everything else is bonus points.

GETTING OFF TO A HEAD START

Most people take a while to ramp up when they start a new job. There's an expected ramp up period before a new hire is expected to do anything of use or value. A secret of the pros is that rather than show up and get familiarized on the job, they use their transition time to get started before they're scheduled to officially get started. They find out what's going on and how they can be useful ahead of time, so that when the new job starts they literally hit the ground running.

The simplest way to get off to a head start is call your new manager and ask what you can do to most effectively prepare for your new job. Say something to the effect of, "Hi, boss. I'm really looking forward to joining the team next week. I've carved out time over the next few days to refresh my skills and start digging into things that will help me get off to a fast start. Where would you suggest I focus my time and attention?"

Don't say, "I'm thinking about preparing," or "I may have a little time to prepare." That's weak. Say, "I'm going to be preparing," or "I'll be refreshing my skills," or "I'm going to get started a little ahead of schedule."

If you give them a chance, the average person is likely to say, "You know what, don't worry about it. Enjoy your down time and relax. There will be plenty of time for work once you get started." Consciously or unconsciously that's exactly what you'll be hoping for. Take the lazy option out of the equation by making a definitive statement of what you WILL be doing.

Once you've made your intentions clear, the new boss will probably offer a suggestion or two on where you can focus your time and attention. If they don't give a solid answer, go back to the original job description and make a judgment call on where your time would best be invested.

You aren't going down the easy road, but you're also not looking to waste time or energy on extraneous activity. If you're going to prepare, do it intelligently. Either way, this is one of a hundred little moments that can help you differentiate yourself from the competition and leap forward as a professional.

FAST TRACK CHALLENGE:

Talk to your future boss and find out what you can do to prepare for the new job. If you aren't in the middle of a career change, talk to your current boss and find out where you can make the biggest contribution your team, department, or company. Then do it.

SOLIDIFYING YOUR REFERENCES

A rock solid reference list is an unparalleled tool for job search, career growth, and professional acceleration. That much is common knowledge. What you might be surprised to learn is that very few people actually have one, and that many job seekers struggle to produce even one top notch reference.

Even strong performers often have a hard time in the reference department, mostly because almost no one makes a consistent *habit* of gathering and solidifying their references. Fewer still take the initiative to find out what the people on their list will say about them when someone calls asking.

The quality of your reference list can easily mean the difference between landing great a job and getting passed over for another applicant (or securing an outstanding salary rather than a mediocre one). Just as important, building your reference list doesn't have to wait until you're facing a transition or starting to look for a new job. That's the most common and least practical time in which to make it happen. A far better practice is to have your references stacked up and ready to go long before you need them. Be proactive about gathering references and recommendations whenever you have the opportunity to do so. Testimonials, letters of recommendation, and the contact details of manager and peer level coworkers can all serve your purpose, and each can be collected at just about any point in time. Gather them in advance and you won't have to go scrambling when they're actually needed. A couple easy ways to ensure you're ready when an opportunity comes knocking include:

1) Proactively write letters of recommendation for the individuals from whom you would like to receive a positive reference in return. Do this without expectation of getting something back from them, but with the knowledge that most people will return the favor without a great deal of arm twisting. A sample letter might look something like this.

2.6 SAMPLE LETTER 1

To Whom It May Concern,

Thank you for the opportunity to recommend Belinda Thomas as a potential project manager for your organization. Simply put, Belinda is outstanding! Over the past five years she has consistently impressed me with her extraordinary capacity to successfully see projects through to completion - even when working with extreme challenges and limited resources.

Belinda is one of the most competent and efficient professionals I've ever worked with, and constantly surprises me with her ability to produce results. She also happens to be extremely pleasant, motivated, and focused, and is a genuine joy to work with. I can't possibly recommend her highly enough and wish I were in a position to hire her myself.

Best regards,
Pamela Green
Executive Vice President

2) Write letters of recommendation about yourself and ask your references to sign them (perhaps excluding your current boss if you think that might raise red flags). You'll have to get over any discomfort you may have over writing about yourself in a positive way, but so long as the recommendation is reasonably on point, you've got a strong chance of them saying yes—especially since you just saved them the time of writing it.

2.7 SAMPLE LETTER 2

Dear Sir or Madam,

Please allow me to take this opportunity to recommend James Wilcox as a staffing industry executive. James has reported to me for five of the past nine years, and worked at an executive level since 2007. Over that time he consistently demonstrated the ability to create strategy, implement policy, deliver world-class training, and provide day to day leadership to our sales and recruiting staff.

James brings a unique understanding of the staffing industry that allows him to communicate effectively with recruiters, account managers, clients, business partners and candidates alike. The combination of skills makes James a valuable asset, and I would recommend him for any position that requires an entrepreneurial spirit and executive level experience.

Best regards,
John Davis
Chief Executive Officer

3) Write a similar letter for past peers and coworkers to sign. The letters should be different for each person, with each reflecting the particular nature of the relationship and experience you had working together. Reference specific projects, accomplishments, and achievements, and follow the same guidelines outlined above. Say nice things about yourself, but be reasonable and on point.

2.8 SAMPLE LETTER 3

Dear Sir or Madam,

Thank you for allowing me the opportunity to recommend Bill Smith. Bill is one of the best executives in the finance industry, and I've had the pleasure of working with him for almost a decade. Bill initially worked with me as a financial controller and consistently performed at a very high level, and his track record of excellence continued as he progressed through the leadership ranks.

I was particularly impressed with his performance through a series of highly complicated mergers a few years back. His ability to recognize important details, spot discrepancies, and use financial data to negotiate better business deals is extraordinary. His work in developing and executing policy, strategy, and day to day operational initiatives has made a significantly positive impact on our company, and I can recommend him with confidence.

Best regards,
Gary Childs
Chief Information Officer

4) Make a deal with colleagues with whom you've enjoyed a good relationship and commit to serving as front line references for each other. Pick people you trust and respect, and make a pact that you'll have each other's back when it comes time to provide references to prospective employers. Check in with them from time to time to make sure you have their most up to date contact details.

5) If you've got serious chops, consider asking your references what they'll

say about you. This takes guts, but if you're willing to go out on a limb, you'll get a pretty good idea of who you really want serving as your primary references. Once a person shares with you what they intend to say, they're unlikely to send a significantly different message to a potential employer.

6) A less intimidating method of validating the quality of your references is to partner with a recruiter or career coach and ask them to make calls on your behalf. You'll get a direct and honest perspective about what your references will say about you without any of the fluff or embellishment they might give when talking to you one on one. You'd be surprised at how many people provide references with nothing positive to say on their behalf. It's not good for the ol' career prospects when your own references sell you down the river, so take the initiative and make sure it doesn't happen.

FAST TRACK CHALLENGE:

Make a list of three or four people whom you can confidently recommend and write letters of recommendation for them. You can choose whether or not to ask for one in return.

HANDLING PERSONAL BUSINESS

This may sound like a very minor point, but handling personal business and completing unresolved tasks can take a huge weight off your shoulders and free up a ton of mental energy. This is useful any time, and especially practical as you prepare to start a new job. Imagine all the new things you have to learn—job duties, tasks, company culture, personality types, names, routines, etc. That's an enormous load for your brain to handle, so the more free space you can clear the better.

Personal business can include anything from doctor's appointments to car repairs, hair cuts, unpaid bills, parking tickets, a cluttered living space or garage, or even a long overdue bath for the family dog. Anything that's hanging over your head and needs to get done. If it comes to mind now, it's something to add to your list and get handled. The fewer "to do" items on your mind, the more bandwidth you'll have available for focusing on delivering outstanding results.

FAST TRACK CHALLENGE:

Create a quick checklist to map out the personal items you can handle in the next two weeks. When you're finished writing, take action and get them done.

Personal Items to Handle: By When:

1)

2)

3)

4)

5)

6)

7)

8)

9)

10)

PART III
GETTING ON THE FAST TRACK

A TALE OF TWO CAREERS

*"The Master of the art of living makes little distinction
between his work and his play, his labor and his leisure,
his mind and his body, his education and his recreation, his
love and his religion. He hardly knows which is which. He
simply pursues his vision of excellence in whatever he does,
leaving others to decide whether he is working or playing. To
him he is always doing both."*

James Michener

❧

I first met Tom and Brian at a Los Angeles chapter meeting of the Project Management Institute in early 2001. The friends had recently graduated from UCLA and started their careers as management consultants with competing firms in the Los Angeles area. Both smiled easily and spoke with confidence, and there was a sense that success was a foregone conclusion for each of them. When the meeting wrapped up we chatted for a few minutes, exchanged business cards, and promised to keep in touch.

We did, and about two years later Brian and Tom found themselves up for promotion at almost exactly the same time. Both were competing with the select group of colleagues who had risen to the top of their respective hiring classes, but despite the tough competition, each felt extremely confident they'd win out over their peers.

A few weeks later I called Brian to check in, hoping to be among the first to offer congratulations. I got his voicemail. The same thing happened when I reached out to Tom. Over the next few weeks I tried each of them a handful of times, but never managed to connect with either. I hoped they'd gotten their promotions and were too busy to respond, but the longer it went without hearing back, the less likely that seemed. After a final attempt a few months later, their cards made it into a stack in my desk drawer for future follow-up and my attention shifted to more pressing business.

Almost six years later I was doing some spring cleaning at the office and stumbled across a stack of old business cards wrapped up in a rubber band. At the very top were the cards Brian and Tom had handed me at our first meeting. Curious about how they were doing, I decided to call and catch up. I tried Tom first. The cell number was disconnected and the receptionist at his old office said there was no longer anyone at the company by that name.

More than half a decade had slipped by since our last conversation, so I wasn't at all surprised to find that Tom had moved on. Undeterred, I took it as a challenge to find out where he'd landed and track him down. Before long we were on the phone together.

As we started to catch up it was clear that Tom wasn't the same guy I'd met all those years ago. Although he had just recently started his fifth job in as many years, he was already talking about the short-sighted management team and how they were the reason for the imminent failure of the project he was leading. I listened to him vent for a while then steered the conversation further into the past, curious to see what had happened with the promotion back at the first company.

Tom had worked his tail off to win the promotion, just as expected. He went for it all out, putting in extra time on his projects, working weekends, and spending hours in preparation for the interviews. He bought a new suit, polished his shoes, and felt great about how things had gone in his meeting with the partners and practice managers. He did everything he could do to the best of his ability, but when the decision came in, the opportunity went to someone else.

He didn't say it in as many words, but it was clear Tom had been crushed by the decision. And it got worse from there. The position had gone to a colleague whose Alma Mater was the same as the managing director who made the final decision. Unable to consider that he'd been beaten fairly, Tom decided the whole thing was rigged, that it had been a decision based on politics rather than performance. He "realized" then and there that going the extra mile would only result in more frustration and disappointment, and decided not to do that any more.

Tom was talented and smart, so even his "B" game was good enough to satisfy the majority of his clients and keep the management team off his back. He kept on working, and since no one commented or complained, he thought no one noticed the drop in performance and attitude.

It didn't click that he was shooting himself in the foot until the next promotion opportunity came up and he was passed over again—this time for someone from the hiring class behind his. He was furious. First shot down for politics (he said) and then snubbed for a junior member of the team. Tom decided it was time to look for a new job. A few months later he accepted a position with a smaller firm, turned in his resignation, and moved into a new job with a bigger salary and expanded responsibilities.

Hoping a fresh start would help him get back on track, Tom threw himself into his work again. This time he was in over his head and struggled to meet the heightened expectations of the new firm. They'd hired with the expectation of getting senior-level performance, and Tom hadn't yet gained that level of experience. The company didn't have the resources to close the skill gap, and Tom was replaced by a more seasoned consultant less than a year later.

He took this loss just as hard as the first one, only this time he blamed the firm for not providing the training and support he needed to perform up to expectations. Over the next few years a pattern emerged. Tom was fired from or quit each of his subsequent jobs, and each time he had a reason or excuse for why things didn't work out. As expected, it was always about the manager, company, or environment—never himself.

Toward the end of our conversation I asked about Brian. They'd mostly lost touch, though Tom still received a Christmas card every year. He graciously gave me Brian's updated contact details before we wished each other well and hung up the phone.

When I reached Brian the story couldn't have been more different. Although his voice sounded deeper, he answered the phone with the same positive energy and enthusiasm I remembered. He apologized for losing touch, and after we'd caught up a little, he shared what had happened in the years since we'd last connected.

Like Tom, Brian had been passed over for that first promotion. He'd put everything he had into landing the opportunity and was heartbroken when it didn't come through. He told me that he'd brooded and moped for the better part of a month, still showing up for work but no longer certain about his commitment to the company or confident about achieving his goals for the future. He avoided calls from friends and family (and me), embarrassed to admit he had "failed."

After weeks of commiserating with Tom about their shared misfortune and the injustice of a corrupt system, Brian picked up the phone and called his dad. His dad, a seasoned technology executive himself, listened to his son for a while before asking a question that would change his trajectory forever. "I'm sorry you didn't get the promotion," he said, "but are you going to let that stop you from achieving the rest of your goals as well?"

Brian paused for a minute, but the answer was obvious. No. He wasn't. Absolutely not.

"Okay, great," his dad said. "Now what are you going to do different so you don't get passed over again next time?"

They brainstormed together for hours, and eventually a roadmap emerged. The next Monday Brian went in to the office and asked his boss if he had time to talk. He did, and the two sat down across the table from each other. Brian opened the conversation by thanking his boss for taking the meeting, and assuring him that although he'd been disappointed by the decision, he was still fully committed to the company. He shared his professional goals and asked if his boss would be willing to coach him and make sure he stayed on track.

The answer was a decisive yes. Over the course of the conversation that ensued, Brian learned not only about the interview and promotion process, but also the evaluation criteria and why the other person had been selected for the promotion. Although he was one of the top candidates, he'd been beaten out by a colleague with a stronger academic background and higher marks in customer service. Brian was a close runner-up, but the winner had an MBA and had sold almost half a million dollars more in add-on services to her clients. The combination made for a relatively easy choice.

Although Brian was still disappointed, it felt good to know why he'd lost and understand what he needed to do differently the next time. Just as important, his manager felt renewed confidence in Brian and was happy to invest energy into his success. They set a weekly appointment to brainstorm, strategize, and evaluate performance.

That same night Brian got on the Internet and started researching graduate-level programs in business and leadership, and within a month he had applied for two of the top MBA programs in the area. He put in extra hours whenever necessary and made a practice of proactively soliciting feedback to make sure his work was on track. He also joined Toastmasters to improve his presentation and speaking skills, and even took a sales course to become more proficient at uncovering new business opportunities.

Within three years of that first "failure" Brian completed a graduate degree in Business Management and was consistently pulling the highest customer service rating in his division. In that same time period he was promoted twice and surpassed the woman who beat him out for the first promotion. Over time he developed the highest performance rating in the division, and by year six he was the youngest practice manager in the company.

By the time we spoke Brian was running one of the most profitable teams in the region and was on track to make partner in the next few years. He was a living example of what happens when talent is coupled with hard work and discipline, and I was thoroughly impressed.

THE ART OF ONGOING SUCCESS

"What the caterpillar calls the end, the rest of the world calls a butterfly."

Lao Tsu

The remainder of this book focuses on practices used by Brian and other fast-track professionals to accelerate their way to the top of the corporate world. Several of them—adopting an opportunity mindset, setting goals, and making powerful transitions—were covered earlier in the book and merit further review. The rest represent techniques and strategies derived from individuals whose habits and choices create extraordinary levels of success and abundance. These start with...

CREATING A HALO EFFECT

Halo Effect: a predisposition to admire all of a person's actions, work, etc., because of an estimable quality or action in the past.

Webster's Dictionary

⊛ ⊛ ⊛

Have you ever met someone who made a great first impression but later proved unreliable, untalented, or otherwise disappointing? How about the flip side? Do you remember meeting someone who gave a horrible first impression, but later proved to be completely trustworthy, capable, and awesome? In either situation, how long did it take to recognize that the person wasn't exactly what you first imagined?

Let's face it: everyone falls victim to an inaccurate first impression from time to time. Usually it takes a while to recognize the mistake. Sometimes it's a person who seems great at first only to become a letdown as the relationship progresses, and sometimes it's an individual who seems dull or unimpressive but later proves extraordinary and wonderful.

Far less common is meeting someone who makes a great first impression and still manages to exceed expectations. Such an experience takes that great first impression, wraps it in steel, and locks it in an iron vault. It's a rare and beautiful thing, and forms the foundation of a Halo Effect.

The important question is this: can such an experience be created intentionally? Are there things you can do in your career that will set you up with a glowing halo and help propel you on a trajectory for extraordinary success?

As it turns out, these questions can be answered with a resounding "yes." Consciously or unconsciously, the majority of elite professionals use a handful of common strategies to accomplish these very goals.

ADOPT A WINNING ATTITUDE

Attitude is the universal starting point for success. Fast Trackers possess an intense focus on their goals, an opportunistic and service oriented attitude, and a fundamental belief in their ability to contribute in a positive and meaningful way. The real pros aren't bashful or shy about going after what they want or chipping in and making a difference for others wherever they can. They go out of their way to find out what's important to others and identify where their time and energy will be most valuably invested.

For the best of the best, work is a vehicle that empowers the achievement of personal and professional ambitions. A job isn't just a job. It's an opportunity to stand out, gain skills, and pursue goals and desires.

Fast Trackers know that when they show up for a new job they are perceived as valuable, competent, and trustworthy. If not, they wouldn't have gotten hired. They recognize that starting a new job puts them at a distinct advantage, and that there's a window of opportunity in which they can extend that advantage or risk losing it altogether. Confidence, humility, and results allow them to extend their position and jump solidly onto the fast track.

BE PREPARED TO LEARN

Regardless of how much education, skill, or experience you bring with you to a new job, you really have no idea what a new environment has in store for you until you show up and start working. Having the right skills and being ready to use them isn't where the magic happens. That's a baseline expectation. The magic happens when you're willing to put aside the tendency to know it all and take the initiative to ask questions, listen, and put what you learn into practice.

Real success requires a healthy degree of curiosity, and the start of a new job is a great time to act childlike in a totally grown-up and acceptable way. It's a time when it's okay to say "I don't know," be inquisitive, and take a proactive interest in learning about things that others might take for granted.

Instead of feeling as though you have to be perfect, take advantage of the limited time available to you as "the new guy" (or girl) and discover as much as you can about what makes someone successful *here*. Your boss and colleagues know the character, culture, and idiosyncrasies of your new environment. They can help you navigate the subtle challenges and obstacles, while pointing out hidden gems that might otherwise get missed.

The more you know about what it takes to get things accomplished with specific individuals and groups, the more quickly you'll be able to apply your expertise in an intelligent and productive manner.

When others contribute by offering their advice, take it to heart and put what they recommend practice. When the advice is sound, say thank you. When it isn't, let it go. Let others become invested in your success. Let them say, "I helped that person when they first started." Give them reasons to root for you and hope you do well. Go out of your way to create an environment of appreciation and collaboration rather than one of opposition and competition.

FAST TRACK CHALLENGE:

Today, find someone more seasoned in your workplace and ask for their advice and guidance on a relevant work topic (even if you've been at the company for thirty years). Listen to what they say, express appreciation, and then put their advice into practice.

MAXIMIZE YOUR MEMORY

"If you want to win friends, make it a point to remember them. If you remember my name, you pay me a subtle compliment; you indicate that I have made an impression on you. Remember my name and you add to my feeling of importance."

Dale Carnegie

Calling someone by name has an almost magical power, especially if you're able to do it after only a meeting or two. Name recognition makes people feel acknowledged, appreciated, and known. It's a gift that everyone loves to receive, but few are able to offer with any degree of reliability.

Remembering names can be a challenge, especially when combined with everything else associated with starting a new job. Many people require numerous introductions before they are fully confident in recalling a name on command, so being able to remember and use names quickly provides a great opportunity to make instant connections.

One of the fastest and most effective ways to get a handle on the names of the people in a new work environment is to create and personalize an organizational (org) chart. In this context, a personalized org chart is a visual representation of the physical environment in which you work, complete with names and memorable details of the other individuals around you.

The exercise of creating such a diagram will improve your memory by: 1) forcing you to pay attention; 2) reinforcing what you learn by taking the information and writing it down; and 3) adding associations that trigger name recognition.

A best practice is to start building your org chart during the interview process. Begin by gathering the business cards of everyone you meet. When you leave the interview, write down everything you remember about each person you met—preferably while you're still in the car and the information is fresh. This will help you lock in names and other relevant details, and will serve as a basis for the more complete and detailed chart you'll build later if you land the job.

Here's the complete process for building an org chart and using it to reinforce name recognition:

1. Draw a picture of all the offices, desks, or cubicles in your area. It doesn't have to be pretty, but it helps to have an accurate representation of the physical layout of the office space.

2.   Fill in the names and information of everyone you can. Start doing this by memory and use aids as necessary. You may wish to include details such as:

    a.   Name/nickname

    b.   Hair color, eye color, and other distinguishing physical features

    c.   Title/role

    d.   Any details you remember from your first or most recent conversation

3.   Practice using each person's name at least two times in each of your first few conversations. This will help move the name from your short-term to long-term memory.

That's it. Draw a picture of your environment, fill in the picture with the names and details of your coworkers, and make a habit of using their names on a regular basis. The whole process should only take a few minutes in a small company, and not that much longer in a bigger environment. In either case creating an org chart is a quick and easy way to jump start name recognition and gain rapport with your new colleagues.

FAST TRACK CHALLENGE:

Create a customized org chart on your current, future, or most recent work environment. Do it even if you know the environment intimately and the names of everyone you work with are as familiar as your living room couch. This exercise is designed to strengthen your memory and build the habit of creating environment specific name associations.

BE INTERESTED

"If there is any great secret of success in life, it lies in the ability to put yourself in the other person's place and to see things from his point of view—as well as your own."

Henry Ford

Having a great attitude and remembering names will put you on the right path, but if you want a halo that really shines, it's not enough. You have to take your new connections to a deeper level, and you have to find ways to contribute to the success of the people around you in a productive and tangible manner.

A simple and highly effective method for doing both is asking open-ended questions and listening to what the other person has to say. Being genuinely interested and curious will not only help you connect with the people around you, but also identify opportunities for real contribution.

Most people like talking about themselves and their interests, and work isn't an exception. When you give new colleagues a chance to share about their backgrounds, skills, and experiences, they usually will. As they do, you're quite likely to discover common interests, shared experiences, and specific ways to be of service. The questions don't have to be deep or profound to get a conversation started. In fact, it's better to start light, especially as you're first getting to know someone. Consider questions like:

"So, where did you work before you started here?"

"How long did it take before you moved into your current position?"

"What did you do before this?"

"What's the biggest challenge on your (project, team, department) right now?"

"How long have you been working on _____? How are things going on that?"

"I noticed that you're working on the _____ project. How is that going?"

Getting to know people isn't a race, so don't rush the process and don't force your way through a bunch of questions like someone scratching items off a checklist. Ask questions, shut up, and let the rest unfold naturally. Conversations and relationships will automatically take on a life of their own. When that happens, stay present and look for ways to be helpful. The rest will take care of itself.

FAST TRACK CHALLENGE:

A great way to override the tendency to interrupt or tune out when others are speaking is to listen with a specific goal or intention. This means proactively paying attention for a specific type of content, outcome, or experience (instead of simply waiting your turn to comment or listening passively). In this context, listening becomes a process of exploration and active discovery, and takes on a whole new dimension of reward and enjoyment.

Just for today, choose one of the following listening goals. Make a game of noting how often content and experiences related to that goal show up, and how your conversations are impacted by the quality of your focus and the nature of your intention. For bonus points, repeat this experiment every day for a week and see what happens in your life.

Listening Goals:

- Discovering something extraordinary or exciting.
- Identifying common areas of interest.
- Hearing value in what the other person has to say.
- Finding reasons to feel appreciative.
- Uncovering ways to contribute to their success.
- Letting others make contributions to you.
- Learning something of value about the other person.

EXCEED EXPECTATIONS

"The first step in exceeding your customer's expectations is to know those expectations."

Roy H. Williams

The more you learn about the people around you the easier it will be to contribute to them in a way that makes a genuine difference. It's like shopping for a significant other on Valentine's Day. Most people enjoy a nice box of chocolates, but that doesn't necessarily mean they'd choose the same box that you would. If your intention is to give a gift that makes the other person happy, shopping for what you want doesn't do any good. In order to give a truly outstanding gift, you have to know what *they* like.

The same is true for on-the-job contribution.

Your boss has specific expectations and goals. He or she wants to see things done in a particular way or on a particular schedule. You can do great work, but if what you deliver doesn't meet or exceed expectations, you've missed the mark. It's like buying dark chocolate chews for someone who prefers white chocolate truffles. It may not be a bad gift, but it's not a great one either.

To contribute beyond expectations requires first knowing what they are. Only after you know what's hoped for can you find predictable and reliable ways to do better (the same is true in intimate and personal relationships). This, too, requires asking questions. If you really want to deliver value and make a positive contribution, start by finding out how that contribution should look and feel to the other person. Ask questions like:

"Can you show me an example of what you're looking for?"

"How would you like the finished product to look?"

"What details should be included in the (report, summary, or deliverable)?"

"How would you like that to be presented?"

"Do you have any preference on the presentation format or structure?"

"What key points need to be covered for this project to be complete?"

"Is there anything else you would like to see included with that?"

"Is there anyone else you would like me to consult before getting started?"

"Is there someone else you'd like me to be working with on this?"

"When would you like this to be completed?"

The words "product," "project," and "deliverable" are used interchangeably here to represent any specific type of output you may be required to hand over. If you are an accountant this might be a balance sheet; if you are a sales person it might be a deal report or prospect sheet; if you're a janitor it might be a well-polished floor or sparkling office space. The goal is simple: first to understand expectations, and then to exceed them.

FAST TRACK CHALLENGE:

Complete at least three of the items on this "first week checklist." Most are simple and all can set you up for extraordinary success in your new position. Take this on even if you aren't in a new job.

3.1 – FIRST WEEK CHECKLIST

✓ Clear your schedule so you can be available after hours or on the weekends for your first month on the job. Use this time to get up to speed on your new tasks, help your past employer find a replacement candidate, or do whatever is necessary to get off to a great start.

✓ Bring donuts or bagels for your entire team sometime during your first week on the job. People love food and automatically feel indebted to those who feed them.

✓ Complete all employment documentation, including new hire paperwork, insurance forms, 401K documents, and anything else that needs to be completed to wrap up the "on-boarding" process.

✓ Sit down with your new manager and:

o Ask exactly what he/she wants you to learn in your first month on the job.

o Ask what specific DELIVERABLES they'll be looking for you to complete in your first week / first month on the job.

o Make sure you have a clear picture of their goals and expectations for your performance.

o Identify their most important goals, projects, milestones, deliverables, etc. Start thinking about ways to help make sure these goals are achieved.

o Schedule a "progress report / status check" meeting with your new manager – to be completed within the first month of employment.

✓ Make an Organizational Chart to help remember the names and personal details of the people you'll be working with (see below for more details).

✓ Take time to connect one on one with the 3-5 people with whom you'll be working most closely.

✓ Identify their key objectives / goals.

✓ Start thinking about how you can help them achieve their goals.

✓ Find out what they are expecting from you and how they hope to work together.

✓ Listen and look for clues about their personal interests and ways to connect at a "human" level.

✓ Schedule a lunch with your mentor sometime in the first two to three weeks. In this meeting:

  o Compare notes on your experiences and their recommendations.

  o Get their opinion of your progress and impressions from the rest of the team.

  o Ask for suggestions or coaching on how to improve in any areas possible.

TAKING INTELLIGENT INITIATIVE

"We must not, in trying to think about how we can make a big difference, ignore the small daily differences we can make which, over time, add up to big differences that we often cannot foresee."

Marian Wright Edelman

❧

Brian's career didn't really take off until he identified what the stakeholders in his company considered valuable and used that information to take well-informed and practical action. Making time to ask questions and gather information is the first part of taking intelligent initiative. Translating the input and information received into action is the second. It's the combination that will differentiate you from the competition and put you on the fast track for career success.

Most people who think of themselves as "go-getters" demonstrate their can-do attitude by taking on more than they can handle, putting in extra hours, and working themselves ragged. This shows initiative but fails the test of intelligence. The test of intelligence dictates that *the only form of initiative likely to be rewarded is that which is perceived as valuable by the other party.*

In this case the other party is a boss, customer, or similarly relevant stakeholder with an active influence over the size of your paycheck and trajectory of your career. You can work yourself silly with eighty-hour weeks and no rest on Sunday, but if you aren't delivering value in the mind of those around you,

you're missing the boat. You would be better off working half the hours with 100 percent of your focus on the handful of actions that will really make a difference to the people around you.

If you really want to know what makes a difference for others, the best way to find out is to ask. Ask your boss their biggest worry, concern, fear, or opportunity. Find out what keeps them up at night, and then find a way to mitigate or eliminate that issue. Ask your customers what they want or need but aren't currently getting, and then find a way to give it to them.

Another great idea is to go out of your way to ask for work. Volunteer to help on additional projects. Find ways to ease the stress and pain of the people around you. Doing more than what's required of you may go against the natural instinct to avoid extra effort, but the result is a lot better than the alternative. When you proactively ask for work you're likely to get the type you actually enjoy. If you wait for work to be given to you, you'll get whatever is left over by your more assertive counterparts.

Don't wait, and just as importantly, don't guess. Making assumptions is like diving headfirst into a pool before checking the depth of the water. You might get lucky, but that doesn't mean it was a good idea. Find out what is important, and then find a way to deliver. It's that simple.

A FEW EXCEPTIONS

In an employment context, there are a few exceptions to the usual "no assumptions" rule. The for-profit business world has a number of common goals and guidelines, including a few that are almost universally safe to pursue without worrying about negative consequences. These dictate that, provided your methods are legal, you may always bring additional revenue to the organization, reduce costs without diminishing profitability, and perform your tasks as well as expected of you or better.

In other words, it is safe to do your job, reduce costs, and increase profits. That's about it (unless you like diving headfirst into untested water, of course).

Among the commonly accepted methods for achieving these ends are a few ideas you may want to test out. These include:

- Finding a high-priority project and helping bring it to a successful conclusion (provided this does not interfere with the successful completion of your assigned duties).

- Expanding profit margins, generating sales, or both (contributing to the bottom line always does your career a favor).

- Identifying inefficient business practices and implementing better ones.

- Engaging in education geared towards improving your skill set and expanding your ability to provide value (e.g. - training, certification, or degree programs).

- Joining industry or trade associations. Professional groups are great sources of information, credibility, connections, and education.

- Reading business books or trade publications directly relevant to your profession. The more knowledgeable you become, the greater your ability to provide value.

Each of these strategies has been tested and proven time and time again. They produce positive results because they make a difference in a way that is recognized and accepted as valuable in the business world. They also require a combination of input and action—input into what's important, and action toward getting it done.

When you see a way to improve efficiency in your business (especially one that doesn't increase risk or cost money), take action and do it. You may catch some heat for not asking permission, but if you demonstrate a bottom-line impact you'll rarely hear anything but muted grumbling. More likely you'll receive praise and commendation. Bosses love being able to take credit for good ideas, and sometimes they get to take credit for the initiative of their subordinates. That's fine. The better your boss does as a result of your efforts, the more likely they are to help you in return.

<u>Fast Track Challenge:</u>

1)   Identify one opportunity to reduce costs, improve revenue, or help with a high-priority project. Without asking permission, take initiative and get it done.

OR

2)   Use the following action plan:

   a.   Ask your boss where you can make the biggest short-term contribution to your team, department, or company.

   b.   Summarize what they tell you and confirm that what you've heard is the same as what they intended.

   c.   Figure out what you need to do to produce the desired outcome.

   d.   *Schedule time into your calendar and create specific action items* that will help you meet or exceed this expectation or goal.

   e.   Stay focused and deliver results.

PRESENTING YOUR IDEAS IN DOCUMENT FORM

"Documentation is like sex: when it is good, it is very, very good; and when it is bad, it is better than nothing."

Dick Brandon

❦

From time to time you may identify an opportunity to make a major contribution that would require an investment of time, money, or energy beyond what you are able to authorize on your own. In these cases it's not a good idea to jump in and take action – not without higher level approval anyway. It's an equally bad idea to throw your ideas out there and hope they will be implemented and credited to you. You might get lucky, but that's not usually how things happen.

Presenting ideas verbally is like tossing pearls in front of the proverbial swine. What you put out is likely to get trampled on or gobbled up, and neither outcome is all that good for you. Sharing an idea verbally without written backup diminishes the perceived value to your audience and simultaneously decreases the odds that you'll get credit even if the idea makes a major difference.

A much more effective approach is to put together proposals that clearly document your ideas and demonstrate the potential benefits of following your advice. Tangible documents can't be as easily dismissed as the spoken word, and the ideas can't be readily snatched away by counterparts with short-term memory or integrity issues. Clear documentation makes your ideas more useful to others, and by extension, more valuable to you.

If you've never created a written proposal before, go to your favorite search engine and run a query on "business presentation template," "business proposal template," or some variation on that theme. The results will include examples and templates that can be adapted and modified to fit your purposes.

A key point in creating high-impact documentation is to give credit where credit is due. You're far more likely to gain support for your proposal if multiple people get behind it. Acknowledging the other people whose ideas influenced your thinking can help make that happen. An added benefit is that generously sharing credit creates an atmosphere in which others are far more likely to acknowledge your contributions in return.

Fast Track Challenge:

Create a proposal that outlines an idea for making a tangible improvement for your employer (or draft a sample business proposal if you're unemployed).

SOLICITING FEEDBACK

"I remind myself every morning: Nothing I say this day will teach me anything. So if I'm going to learn, I must do it by listening."

Larry King

࿇

B rian discovered early in his career that feedback is the lifeblood of progress. He learned that the input given him by clients and leadership had a direct impact on his professional success, and that the more effectively he integrated input into performance, the more quickly his career moved forward.

In the context of work, there are two basic ways to get feedback. One is to passively wait for someone to give it to you (e.g. - in a scheduled monthly, quarterly, or annual review). The other is to proactively look and ask for it as a matter of habit.

On the job, as in life, it pays to be proactive.

Instead of assuming you know what your boss wants, ask what he or she wants. Instead of assuming your performance is on or off target, ask the individuals affected by your work whether it is. Find out what is really going on rather than making assumptions. When in doubt, go out of your way and ask.

The practice of asking for feedback can be a bit uncomfortable, especially at first. After all, most of us are accustomed to waiting passively for others to provide input rather than actively looking for it (mostly due to the fear of criticism). It's okay to be afraid, so long as the fear doesn't stand in the way of taking action. Fear is natural; courage is stepping up and doing it anyway.

Developing courage is a reward in and of itself, but the simple fact is that constructive criticism and negative feedback provide information that is far more valuable than positive reinforcement. Positive reinforcement is great, especially when you're really working at full throttle, but it doesn't help you get better. Criticism stings, but provides a clear opportunity for improvement.

Imagine, for example, that you are working on a particularly important project. You're going about your business and feel like things are going okay. You're getting your assignments done on time and consider the work you're doing to be completely acceptable. Your boss, on the other hand, is unhappy with your performance. They think you could be performing at a much higher level and are quietly disappointed by your efforts.

Imagine further that you don't go out of your way to ask for feedback and simply continue doing your job at exactly the level you are right now. At what point will you find out your manager is unhappy?

If you work for an unusually competent leader you may be fortunate enough to have a side conversation where the issue gets addressed one on one. That's if you're lucky. More likely the issue will come out in a team meeting or during a formal performance review. If it comes out in a team meeting it will be embarrassing for you and may damage your relationship with your manager and peers. Not ideal. If you wait until an official review, you may be put on a performance plan, fired, or miss out on the possibility of a pay increase, promotion, or other positive reward. Again, no one wins.

Now imagine that you're in that same situation. You're working along and thinking things are going just fine. This time instead of assuming you're okay, you make the effort to ask for feedback—just to be sure. You sit down with your boss one on one and ask how you're doing. As the conversation develops, it comes out that your performance is way off target. You're perceived as a slacker, have misunderstood instructions, aren't communicating effectively, or have made some critical mistake of which you're totally unaware. One way or another, things aren't going nearly as well as you thought they were. Bad news, right?

Maybe, but maybe not. The conversation may become awkward for a moment. Probably will. Criticism can hurt a bit, and you might find yourself getting defensive or feeling upset. You were hoping for positive feedback and affirmation, and instead you're on the receiving end of tongue lashing. You may wish you'd never brought the subject up at all, but that's short-sighted. The exceptionally positive news is that you now have a chance to improve your performance and address the situation *proactively*.

Instead of the issue blowing up at a meeting or coming out in a performance review (at which point it's too late), you can immediately go to work on adjusting whatever is necessary to deliver at the level that's expected of you. Assuming you're willing to make such an effort, you have a shot at being perceived as someone who takes initiative and is able to deal with constructive criticism. It also shows that you're capable of doing what is necessary to produce results. Think that might have an impact on the outcome of your next performance review? Darn right it will.

Proactively seeking feedback doesn't have to be confined to your manager, either. You can ask questions of your colleagues, subordinates, clients, family, and friends. The more feedback you gather, the more effective you will become at contributing, delivering value, and having a positive impact on the various people you serve (within reason, of course).

Fast Track Challenge:

This week, ask three people for feedback on your performance—two from work and one from your personal life. Ask each of them how you're measuring up to expectations and request that they offer one suggestion on a specific area in which you could improve (make it clear that one is enough for now). Take the information they give you and put it to the best use you can.

BUILDING A CAREER PORTFOLIO

"When your work speaks for itself, don't interrupt."

Henry J. Kaiser

☙❧

In Part II we talked about Greg, the candidate who successfully landed an offer 10 percent above the company's target pay scale *without* having to negotiate or play games. While many factors contributed to his success, one of the most powerful tools in his arsenal was a stunning career portfolio. Instead of answering questions with words, he used his portfolio to address questions with clear examples of the outcomes produced through his efforts.

On top of great interview skills and a solid resume, Greg's ability to demonstrate his expertise with visual examples separated him from all of the other candidates he competed against in the interview process. The combination influenced the decision makers to such an extent that they ponied up serious money to become his employer of choice.

Ultimately, that is the goal of portfolio building—to demonstrate your skills and experiences in a way that makes it easy for current and future employers to quantify the value you can provide to them. A high-caliber portfolio is a clear pathway to creating value propositions that produce bottom line results for your career and income.

Portfolio building is exactly what you'd expect it to be. It is the process of creating a physical or visual representation of the work that you do - just like the portfolio created to showcase the work of an artist or writer. In the context of a career portfolio, this will include three basic types of documentation: work samples, credibility boosters, and testimonials.

WORK SAMPLES

Work samples are the heart of a career portfolio. This is where you get to show off who you are and what you're capable of doing in a way that people in your field will recognize and appreciate. The samples may be presented in numerous formats, all with the intention of showing a tangible representation of your work (written, visual, digital, and so on). You can take pictures, capture screen shots, print images, make copies, or even create new samples to showcase your skills and abilities.

A beautifully washed and detailed Ferrari is the perfect endorsement for the work of an auto spa. A code sample or application screen shot is appropriate for a software engineer. A picture of a brilliant smile full of bright white teeth is right on target for an orthodontist. The specific type of documentation should be appropriate to your industry and profession, and the examples should be demonstrative of your very best work.

CREDIBILITY BOOSTERS

Credibility boosters are bits of information that demonstrate expertise and are designed to positively influence the thinking of your audience. Examples can include college and university diplomas, relevant certifications, skills test results, educational transcripts, proofs of membership, and so on. Anything that demonstrates you are plugged in, knowledgeable, or proactively involved in your industry is appropriate in this section. Diplomas, memberships, and certifications are always a good idea, but you should only include transcripts and test results if they reflect high marks.

TESTIMONIALS

The inclusion of testimonials is an extremely effective way to validate and support the legitimacy of other documentation shown in your portfolio. Testimonials "prove" that you are, in fact, an excellent resource. These can come in the form of letters of recommendation, professional references, client acknowledgements, and even copies of thank-you letters and emails. The more people who say good things about you, the better, so include as many testimonials as you can.

PUTTING IT ALL TOGETHER

A portfolio is all about showcasing your work in a way that is helpful and impressive to your target audience. The goal of a portfolio is the same as that of a resume—to make it easy for your audience to say yes to you.

In either physical or digital format, a career portfolio needs to be readily accessed and navigated during an interview, and should include content that is both relevant and visually appealing. The materials should be neatly organized in a format that lends itself to simple demonstration and review.

A three-ring binder with navigation tabs is a low-cost yet highly effective tool for creating a physical version of your portfolio. Organization and navigation are easy, and the binder is a presentation format familiar to almost everyone in the civilized world. For an extra touch of awesomeness, upgrade to a leather-bound version.

Blogs offer one of the easiest and most cost-effective ways to create an online version of your portfolio. The two dominant blog services on the market are Blogger (Google's www.blogger.com) and WordPress (www.wordpress.com). Both are free to use and highly effective for hosting and presenting information, as are many of the smaller blog services on the market.

A blog allows you to upload and display documents, images, links, code samples, video, articles, posts, photos, and more, enabling you to build a robust portfolio at literally no cost. More sophisticated technologists (and those willing to spend a couple bucks) can customize a blog to resemble a website, adding a more personalized look and feel to their online portfolio.

INTERVIEW TIP

When using a portfolio in an interview, be cognizant of the fact that not everyone wants to see work samples. Some people are more interested in conversation, so before you start showing off your work, ask whether the person would prefer to see examples or hear explanation.

BIG BANG STRATEGY

As you construct your portfolio, consider putting it together in a way that reflects the type of work you do. A project manager, for example, could build their portfolio in the same way they would document and manage a project. It might start with a sample project charter, move into a project plan, include scope, budget and timeline estimates, walk through milestone reports, and finish with a summary of deliverables, metrics reports, or other outcomes.

It could include copies of relevant certifications, testimonials from satisfied employers and customers, letters of recommendation, references, appreciative emails, and anything else that demonstrates a high level of skill and experience. These materials should be organized intuitively and logically to make it easy to find each relevant document and work sample. The more organized and professional-looking your portfolio, the more positive the impact it will have on prospective employers.

The same structure applies regardless of skill set or profession. A Web developer could include documentation through the life cycle of the development process. It might start with requirements documentation, move into wireframes or a story board, include a few strings of sample of code, and conclude with screen shots of the completed site.

Someone working in the world of tangible, physical products can create a compelling portfolio by highlighting their work through photographs, sketches, and renderings. A craftsman can demonstrate their product in various stages of completion and write details about their role in bringing it through to a finished state. Testimonials, letters of recommendation, industry affiliations, certifications, educational documents, and thank-you emails are applicable in every situation.

FAST TRACK CHALLENGE:

Spend an hour or two gathering as many work samples, testimonials, and credibility boosters as you can easily find. Use this as a starting point for constructing a tail-kicking career portfolio, and follow the guidance in the next section to round out the missing details.

FILLING GAPS IN A PORTFOLIO

If you find yourself in the position of having a great deal of experience but very few relevant supporting documents (or very little experience and subsequently few supporting documents) it can be daunting to recognize how much work it will take to build a robust portfolio.

Unfortunately, there aren't a lot of shortcuts that fall on the right side of the ethical line. If you want to build a high-quality portfolio and don't currently have the documents or credentials, it's going to take some time and effort to fill in the gaps. Don't let that discourage you. A career spans decades, and you can add a lot of great content to a portfolio in a relatively short period of time.

To that end there are a number of great ways to ethically and professionally accelerate the process of portfolio building. These same techniques are extremely effective at filling gaps in a resume and providing value to your community. Among the easiest and most consistently effective are volunteering, creating a passion project, and reconnecting with past employers.

STRATEGIC VOLUNTEERISM

Volunteering is great because it serves so many purposes at the same time. There are literally thousands of charities and not-for-profit organizations that could benefit from your personal and professional skills (regardless of what they happen to be), and there's a very good chance of finding one within a few minutes of your home.

Volunteering provides an opportunity to make a difference for people in genuine need of assistance, and simultaneously affords great opportunities to generate work samples, gain experience, and pick up professional recommendations. Work done in a not-for-profit context is valid professional experience whether or not you get paid. That's one of the great benefits of a portfolio. It's impossible to argue with the physical proof of well-documented work activities, especially when that work is accompanied by testimonials.

If you're lucky (and smart), your volunteer work will overlap with the next option and you'll find a charity that coincides with your personal passions or hobbies. In addition to fleshing out your portfolio and making a difference, you may also have some fun in the process. If you don't know where to start, visit www.charitynavigator.org or www.charityfinders.com to identify a worthy cause in your area.

CREATE A PASSION PROJECT

"When work, commitment, and pleasure all become one and you reach that deep well where passion lives, nothing is impossible."

Author Unknown

What drives and motivates you to get through the work week? What do you look forward to, think about, and anticipate jumping into as soon as you set foot outside of the office? What do you do for fun when nobody is paying your salary and nothing is on the line? Do you enjoy bike riding, hiking, climbing, movies, crime dramas, eating, drinking, sleeping, talking, cars, motorcycles, collectibles, or supporting a specific cause?

Creating a passion project allows you to use what you enjoy as an opportunity to showcase your professional skills. A Web developer with a love for gourmet food could build a beautiful website designed to showcase their favorite cuisine and recipes. An engineer with a passion for cycling could design a low-cost bike for the underprivileged. An accountant could volunteer their services to a favorite charity or not-for-profit organization and help get their books in order.

Anyone can use a passion project as an opportunity to have fun and create tangible documentation of their work. It's a great excuse to build a project plan, design a website, write a blog, organize a team, come up with a creative solution to a social problem, or showcase your talents in a thousand different ways. The range of possibilities is nearly infinite, and all it takes is a little creativity and initiative to get started.

TIME TRAVEL

We are all served better by looking to the future than dwelling on the past, but there are times when the products of earlier days can be quite helpful. A portfolio is a great example. The probability is that you have, at some point in your career, done a spectacular piece of work to which you no longer have access and wish that you did. It happens to everyone sooner or later.

Unfortunately, traveling back in time to recapture the fruits of your labor isn't an option. Sad but true. You can, however, connect with past colleagues and bosses and ask for their help in building your portfolio. They can assist by writing letters of recommendation, providing supporting documentation about the nature of the work you did, and sometimes even digging up work samples that might otherwise have been lost to you for good.

Reach out to the people with whom you have shared your career. Tell them what you're up to, and ask for their help. If you're genuine, there's a good chance of finding at least one person willing to support you in your endeavors. Some may even get inspired to build their own career portfolio, in which case you can return the favor and help them get started in return. Reaching out to people from the past is a great way to fill gaps in a portfolio and a great excuse for reconnecting with your best business associates. That's a winning combination no matter how things work out, and it's not at all uncommon for such connections to lead to future job offers.

FAST TRACK CHALLENGE:

Come up with a passion project designed to serve a not-for-profit organization. Pick something that allows you to leverage the professional strengths you wish to highlight in your job search. An ideal project is one that has the potential to make a real-world difference and provide genuine enjoyment. Once you have a project, start documenting your work, invite friends and colleagues to play along, and have a great time.

BUILDING YOUR PROFESSIONAL NETWORKS

"Ambitious people climb, but faithful people build."

Julia Ward Howe

༒

The greatest position of power an employee can have is one of being sought after. The real winner of the new employment game is not the person who knows the most tricks for finding and applying for jobs. It's the person who doesn't have to because the jobs come looking for them.

The moment you shift from being a job seeker to being someone who is sought after, you step into a new realm of power and opportunity. That's the real goal of this book, and networking is one of the best tools for making that shift happen.

You are undoubtedly familiar with the term "six degrees of separation" and the premise that you are connected to anyone and everyone alive through your network of existing personal connections. By leveraging all of your connections to the fullest extent, you could theoretically generate a direct personal introduction to Bill Gates, Steven Spielberg, Nelson Mandela, or the Rolling Stones.

Whether or not this proves true in reality is irrelevant. The basic concept is sound. The more people you are directly connected to, the broader your range of total connections and the closer you are to the job, employer, and career of your dreams.

Most companies hire through employee referrals first, trusted recruiters second, and finally from job boards and unsolicited applications. Referrals save time, minimize recruiting costs, and mitigate the risks associated with bringing in an unknown resource.

Unless you are connected to people who can recommend you for a specific position, it's a job you're relatively unlikely to land. Someone who is plugged in to that network is going to get the first shot, and because of their personal connections they'll also have the inside track for getting hired (even if other applicants have comparable skills).

The greater your range of connections, the more likely you are to land one of these "insider" job opportunities. As you can well imagine, eliminating the competition before they become competition is the best possible advantage in any type of contest.

These days there are two primary forms of networking: online or "social networking" and traditional networking. Social networking is an outstanding method of meeting, connecting with, and getting to know other people from around the world in an indirect way. Traditional networking is all about building face-to-face relationships in the real world.

Both forms are invaluable as you grow and manage your career, and each is well worth an investment of time, energy, and sometimes even money. Hard stats are hard to come by, but everyone in the employment game agrees that a high percentage of hiring happens through referrals (a quick online search will reveal statistics that range from as low as 20 percent to as high as 80 percent). That means there's an excellent chance that your next job will come via a recommendation by someone in your direct circle of influence.

"SOCIAL" NETWORKING

Although the old axiom is "six degrees of separation," a healthy online network means you're probably only two or three degrees away from at least one person who holds your dream job in their hands. More than a billion people worldwide are on the Internet today, with more joining by the minute. The number of individuals who have signed up for social and professional networking sites has jumped into the hundreds of millions, including the vast majority of working professionals in the modern world.

Online networking provides fast-track access to almost anyone you may wish to reach, and there are numerous ways to have your "social" networking be productive in a very professional way. The first key is to pick the right places to invest your time and energy.

The list of leading resources is likely to change over time, but current frontrunners for recruiting are LinkedIn and Facebook, with Plaxo, Google+, Twitter and a number of others somewhere in the running. Due to the overt emphasis on professional networking, the majority of this section will be spent on LinkedIn.

LINKEDIN

Over the past few years LinkedIn has become the de facto standard for online professional networking—*professional* being the operative word. LinkedIn is one hundred percent dedicated to connecting and reconnecting people in the working world and is not a venue for "social" networking in the traditional sense.

LinkedIn is for business, not chatting with friends or posting personal information. The site is robust, well-marketed, and highly utilized by business people in most English-speaking countries (and a number of others as well). If you're reading this book, the odds are high that you're already a member.

Although LinkedIn is widely used, job seekers and employers are only beginning to understand the power of the site from a networking and career development standpoint. Everything about LinkedIn has been engineered to provide professional value, and there are numerous features that make it a highly useful resource in many capacities. Among the most important to a

Fast Tracker are Connections, Groups, Discussions, Recommendations, and the Jobs section.

Connections

In the context of LinkedIn, a Connection is a person with whom you can interact directly because one person accepted an invitation from the other. A Connection can be made with anyone who is willing to "link" with you. This usually happens on the basis of a past relationship, shared interest, personal recommendation, or mutual desire to network.

The list is usually made up of current and past colleagues, friends, business partners, and others with whom you share common interests. Invitations to connect can be sent to nearly anyone on the site, provided you have a recommendation from a shared contact, email address, common past employer or educational institution, or are both members in the same LinkedIn Group.

Groups

Much like traditional networking groups, Groups on LinkedIn are communities for people with shared interests, goals, or experiences. The only real difference is that these are virtual and thereby unconstrained by geography. That means you're unlikely to find an in-person gathering, but would be equally hard-pressed to find an unrepresented profession, trade, technology, or business sector.

You can find relevant Groups by running a key word search, and joining is as easy as clicking the button to send a membership request to the group sponsor. In some cases, such as Alumni Groups and those that require a specific certification or skill set, you may be asked to verify your eligibility before being accepted as a member.

On average, however, requests are accepted without question, and you will be given access to the discussion boards, job postings, and online forums associated with that Group. Once you're plugged in, you'll also have access to contacting and networking with all other members. That makes it easy for interested employers to reach you and provides a pathway to rapidly increasing the size of your online network.

Discussions

A great way to build Connections and get noticed as an expert is through participation in the Discussion forums found within the Groups. Discussions are a venue for posing questions, comments, and information relevant to members of that specific community. Posting intelligent questions, answers, and content helps make you visible to people in the Group. That, in turn, makes you a ripe target for recruiters, hiring managers, and HR professionals on the hunt for new talent.

Discussions are also a great forum for gathering insight on hot topics, soliciting help in solving problems, and doing targeted research. A few simple ways to take advantage of the Discussion boards include sharing links to relevant news articles and blogs, posting challenging or thought-provoking questions, responding to questions posed by other members, and sharing samples of your work.

Provided you do all of this in a professional and intelligent way, you will be gaining credibility with an audience that shares your interests and has connections within your industry. You'll also be making yourself visible to those who visit the site for the express purpose of recruiting, which is a great practice if you happen to be interested in exploring new career opportunities.

Recommendations

The Recommendations feature is one of the most exceptional available on LinkedIn. Recommendations allow you the opportunity to write positive feedback about others, have others write positive feedback about you (similar to a traditional letter or recommendation), and to have this information displayed on your profile for all the world to see.

LinkedIn is a professional networking site, so no one can post on your page without permission and you always get a chance to review feedback before it is displayed. This provides an unprecedented opportunity to display positive input and comments about your skills and experience without looking like a braggart. Very few things speak more clearly than the words of others, and in the context of career, testimonials are as good as gold.

A great practice for fully leveraging the Recommendations feature is to proactively write them for everyone you can authentically recommend. Your comments can be short and sweet or long and detailed. It doesn't matter. So long as your recommendation is genuine there is a very strong probability that you will receive one from the other person in return. Layered on top of a well-engineered profile, Recommendations let people know they may have just stumbled across the genuine article.

Jobs

The Jobs section on LinkedIn is exactly what you'd expect it to be—an online directory of career listings submitted by individuals and companies looking to hire. Just like other job boards, these postings can be searched by key word, geography, company, industry, and other relevant parameters.

3.3 LINKEDIN SCREEN SHOT 2[10]

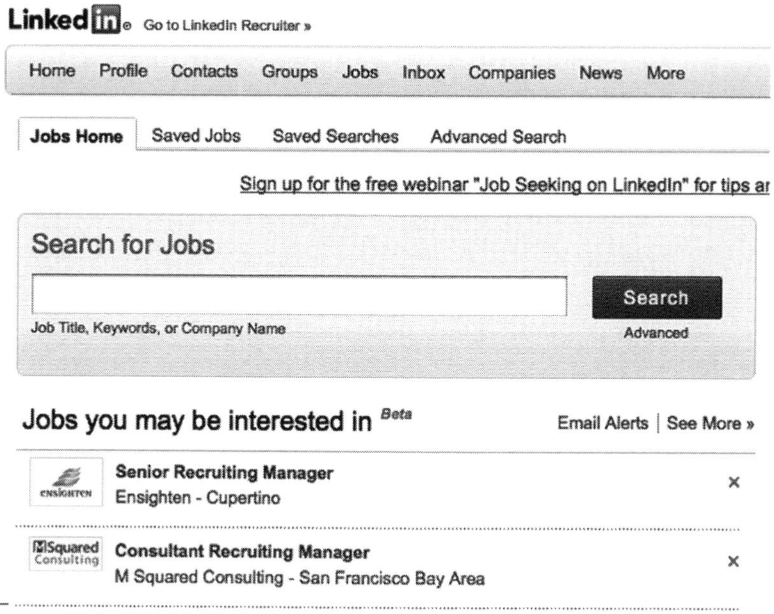

3.4 LINKEDIN SCREEN SHOT 3[11]

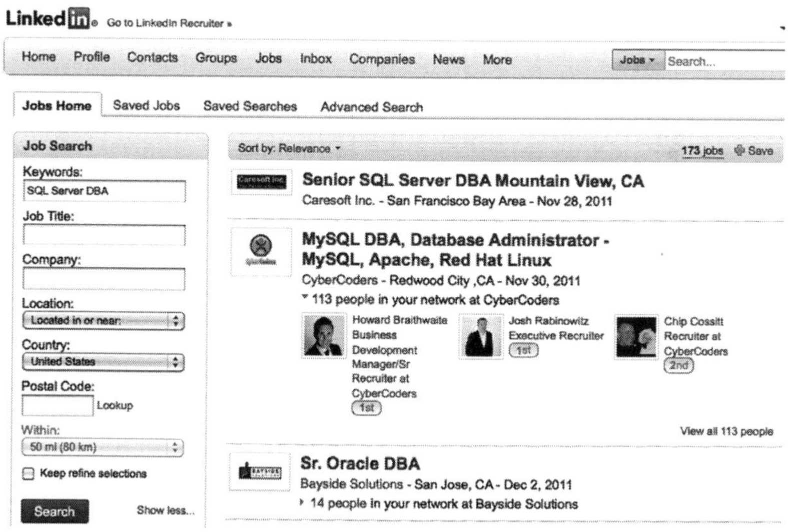

10 Job search interface from www.linkedin.com

11 Job Search results page from www.linkedin.com

There are several distinct advantages to finding openings on LinkedIn that aren't available on any other job search site. For one, the results screen automatically lets you know everyone through whom you're connected to the person who put up the listing. You can proactively ask your Connections for suggestions on the best ways to secure an interview and even get these people to directly recommend you for the position.

This can be a huge competitive advantage, and a great reason to make sure you have a robust profile and lots of positive recommendations on your page. If you get introduced to a hiring manager via LinkedIn, that person is probably going to check you out on the site as well. Make sure they find good reasons to take the suggestion and move you forward into the hiring process.

ONLINE SOCIAL NETWORKING

Facebook, MySpace, Google+, and similar sites aren't really known for professional networking, but they absolutely can be useful in a job search. Most users go to these sites to connect with friends and family, but more and more businesses and professionals are creating profiles, recruiting, advertising, and engaging in business-related activities each and every day.

Just as important, friends and family can be a GREAT resource in your job search *if* they know what you do for a living and that you're looking for work. Social networking sites offer a quick and easy way to let lots of people know you're on the market for a new job and exactly how they can be of help in finding your next position.

One could quickly put up a post to the effect of, "Hey all—just got notice that the company is outsourcing my position next month. Starting today I'm looking for a great new IT Project Manager opportunity in the St. Louis area. Please let me know if you have any suggestions or recommendations (or even better, people I can talk to). Thanks!"

In just a few minutes you can engage dozens or hundreds of personal connections into helping with your job search. That's a very efficient use of time and energy, and you never know where such a simple action might lead.

One clear advantage of social networking is that the people with whom you're associated are likely to help if they can. After all, they're friends, family, and others who have intentionally chosen to connect with you, and that's a great starting point.

A few words of caution…

If you're going to use a social networking site as a professional tool, don't post things you don't want current or prospective employers to find. As a matter of fact, make a habit of not posting anything online that you wouldn't want an employer to see—period.

The number of stories about job seekers on the verge of receiving employment offers only to have them disappear after a review of their social networking profile(s) is rapidly increasing. Inappropriate posts, pictures, and pursuits are commonly used as criteria to screen out high-risk candidates and minimize hiring mistakes. Long story short, don't put anything on your site that you wouldn't want a future boss to see.

Similarly, be cognizant of the people you connect with online. If you have a friend who is prone to inappropriate posts and comments, you might be better served by disconnecting online and reconnecting by phone or in person (or perhaps disconnecting altogether). It may not be fair, but we're all judged by the company we keep. This is as true online as it is in the real world. Use good judgment in both worlds, and you'll be in good shape when leveraging social networks for professional purposes.

TWITTER

Much like social and professional networking sites, Twitter is widely used and helps people keep touch in the modern world. The tool allows simple one-sentence text messages to go out to an entire network. In the context of a job search, that can include things like: "on CareerBuilder looking for IT Project Manager positions in St. Louis," "just had a great interview for an IT Project Manager position here in St. Louis," or "updating my resume and getting ready to look for a new PM opportunity in St. Louis."

If you're in the middle of a great project, you post a quick update. Need a resource, post a quick update. The tool is simple and the idea is simple, but the jury is still out on whether or not Twitter is a genuinely effective tool for the average job seeker. It is, however, an interesting phenomenon in the networking world, so it would be worthwhile to experiment and try to find value for yourself.

TRADITIONAL NETWORKING

"If you're not networking, you're not working."

Denis Waitley

Traditional networking is one of the most valuable and time-tested practices available to job seekers and fast-trackers alike. While social networking provides the advantage of speed and convenience, traditional networking provides an even bigger advantage: real-world relationships with people who share your interests and have the power to make an impact in your own backyard.

In the context of career, the value of traditional networking can't be over-stated. Personal connections are considered more likely to yield your next job offer than any other resource or method, and well-connected people tend to get promoted far more quickly than others. It seems unfair (and probably is), but since it's a fact of the business world, why not use it to your own advantage.

Traditional networking provides opportunities to gain knowledge and expertise, connect with relevant decision makers and influencers, and secure the inside track on unpublished job opportunities. The list goes on from there.

In addition to the advantages to you as a job seeker and professional, it can also be a great source of fun, entertainment, and education. There are countless venues and opportunities for networking in the real world, and most of them can be found with a quick query on your favorite search engine.

NETWORKING VENUES

Whether or not you want to engage in networking, it's unquestionable that building relationships in your field provides advantages and opportunities that outsiders are unlikely ever to see. For that reason, you should make it a habit to attend at least one on-site networking event per month. Here are a few different options you may want to consider:

User Groups:

Found extensively in the technology industry (and many others as well), user groups cater to individuals with experience working with a common tool, technology, product, industry, or field. User groups are a highly useful venue for ongoing education, contacts, and interested employers. They also tend to be rich in visiting recruiters, HR professionals, and hiring managers seeking to identify and attract talent from a very specific pool of resources.

Trade Groups and Associations:

Much like user groups, trade associations exist in every major market for almost every industry and profession in the English-speaking world. These communities attract the attention of all three hiring audiences as well, and are a great source of networking opportunities, education, market information, accreditation, and industry-specific certifications. These are especially useful for networking in niche markets.

Toastmasters International:

Although not formally a "networking" group, Toastmasters offers extraordinary value in professional development and the opportunity to meet great people. The primary emphasis in Toastmasters is on the sharpening of presentation skills and public speaking abilities, and each Club has a unique style and theme. As a result, the meetings tend to attract motivated and like-minded professionals. The combination of networking and professional development creates a fantastic opportunity for career acceleration.

True "Networking" Groups:

There are literally thousands of groups and meetings completely dedicated to the art and science of networking. These can be particularly useful for entrepreneurs, small businesses, network marketers, independent contractors, and individuals looking to promote specific products and services. Among the industry leaders in the area of professional networking are BNI, Leads Club, First Tuesday, and Le Tip, all of which can be found online and are likely to have meetings in your area.

MeetUp Groups:

Meetup.com is a hybrid between social and traditional networking. It's an Internet venue for connecting people with live events and networking opportunities in local markets. The site is a relatively open forum for people with a wide variety of personal and professional interests to find groups of like-minded individuals and get connected with them. Provided you live in a reasonably populated area, you will almost certainly find a relevant Meetup in your local area that gets together on a weekly, bi-weekly, or monthly basis.

GETTING STARTED

For many people the biggest hurdle to networking is getting started. The effort to find a group and consistently show up for the meetings deters the vast majority of professionals. It means going to new places, meeting new people, and, heaven forbid, talking about oneself in front of strangers.

Networking forces most people out of their comfort zone, and that's almost always a good thing. Even though the initial effort can be challenging, most groups are exceptionally generous with new and prospective members. Old-timers go out of their way to help new people feel at home and get value, and the groups as a whole tend to welcome new members with open arms. On average you won't find a safer or more productive venue for getting to know new people than a networking group.

Rather than get stressed about the whole process, pick an appealing venue from the list above, go online to find out the time and date of the next meeting, and then show up. If you can't decide which one to choose, flip a coin or try "eenie meenie, miney mo." It's a common practice to check out a handful of groups before choosing a finalist, so don't worry about getting stuck at the first place you try.

A great practice is to focus on making connections and observing interactions, especially in the first few meetings. Pay attention to the way experienced networkers introduce themselves. Listen to what they say and how they say it. Observe the way they interact with others. When you hear or see something that grabs your attention in a positive way, write it down. You can borrow it later.

You will refine and enhance the way you introduce and talk about yourself over time, so don't worry about getting it "right" at the very beginning. In this context there's really no such thing as right or wrong—just more and less effective. Developing a great presentation style and building your skills as a networker is an ongoing process, and you don't have to spend too much time wrapped up in the details. Pick a group, show up, and decide whether or not you like it. If you do, jump in and become a member. If not, go somewhere else.

Once you've become a member there are really only three things you need to do: 1) show up 2) build relationships, and 3) provide value to others. If you consistently go to meetings, connect with the people you meet, and make a point of being helpful, you're on your way to networking success.

FAST TRACK CHALLENGE:

Identify a networking group, user group, trade association, or Toastmasters Club and visit within the next five business days. Don't think about it. Do it.

FOLLOWING YOUR PASSIONS

"If there is no passion in your life, then have you really lived? Find your passion, whatever it may be. Become it, and let it become you and you will find great things happen FOR you, TO you and BECAUSE of you."

T. Alan Armstrong

❦ ❦ ❦

In Western culture we have a tendency to separate the things we enjoy from the things we do for money. We've taken this to such an extent that business and fun are often considered antonyms ("Is this trip for business or pleasure?"). Unfortunately, that's not a great way to get ahead. The people who thrive in the professional world, the real Fast Trackers, are those who love what they do and get satisfaction out of doing it well. An inspiring vision for the future combined with fun and passion in the present creates a recipe for extraordinary success.

So…what are you passionate about? What do you do when there's nothing you *have to* do? What is the number-one way you spend your time when no one is telling you what to do with it? Think about it for a minute, and then ask yourself the following question:

What skills and attributes have I developed while engaging in this activity?

If your favorite pastime is watching crime dramas, for example, you may find that you've developed a knack for anticipating plot lines and predicting outcomes in places where others get lost in the twists and turns of the storyline. This may seem like a small or inconsequential thing, but analytical and predictive-thinking skills are extremely valuable in a business context.

The more accurately you can predict outcomes in a business setting, the more you can steer your company or team away from mistakes and toward success (if you don't think that's valuable, just ask Warren Buffett, Bill Gates, or Donald Trump). Document your predictions, observe what happens, and when you're confident in your abilities, share your insights with relevant decision makers in your organization.

The same principle applies to almost any area of personal interest. If you are drawn to sports and competition, consider creating games that drive you to higher performance. If your interest is music, integrate some aspect of rhythm, rhyme, beat, or harmony into the way you engage in your work activities. Don't limit your imagination or get stuck in your thinking. With a little creativity, you'll find a way to bring passion into your practice.

FAST TRACK CHALLENGE:

Take a few minutes and write down the unique skills and attributes you have developed through the enjoyment of personal hobbies and pastimes. Identify how these skills apply in a business context and make note of any ideas you have for applying them in a useful and meaningful way.

Example: I love watching crime dramas and have gotten really good at figuring out the twists and turns and predicting the outcomes before they happen. I can apply that skill to analyzing business situations and predicting the likely outcome of a given project or initiative. I can use this talent to help the company steer clear of mistakes and make better business decisions.

My unique skills and how I can apply them:

EXPANDING YOUR POTENTIAL

"Don't judge each day by the harvest you reap, but by the seeds you plant."

Robert Louis Stevenson

❁

W hen it comes to personal development, people usually think about college, seminars, big-name gurus, and other fixed-format training programs. There is value in each of these, no doubt, but that's not the extent of what's available to you. Personal development doesn't have to look or feel any particular way, and it certainly doesn't have to happen in a classroom, seminar or group setting.

Engaging in personal development is the practice of participating in activities that expand who you are and what you're capable of as a person. If you want to find courage, it's probably not going to happen in a classroom. Jump behind the wheel of a race car, step into a kung fu class, bungee jump, speak on stage, skydive, or do something else you find utterly terrifying and you're probably on the right track (and just might have a blast in the process).

Jumping out of an airplane at ten thousand feet may seem unrelated to your day-to-day job. It probably is. The boost in self-esteem, however, is almost certain to spill over into the other areas of your life – work included – and that added touch of confidence might just be the difference between you and another applicant next time you're vying for a job or promotion.

You can't make a significant gain in one area of your life without it affecting the others as well. That's why it's so important to engage in activities that expand and enhance who you are.

There are, of course, many less thrilling forms of personal development that translate more directly into improved business performance. Self-improvement books and seminars absolutely have their place and value. A great book can guide you to let go of disempowering opinions and beliefs, create better habits, inspire productive action, or break through to higher levels of performance.

Business and industry seminars provide education, training, knowledge, and personal connections in a specifically relevant context. College courses, vocational schools, professional certifications, and specialized training programs provide opportunities to improve skills and enhance credibility. Reading relevant news and publications can provide insight into your market, industry trends, and methods of sharpening your skills.

There are countless outlets and avenues for developing any aspect of yourself you wish to focus on and improve. A quick online search will reveal an abundance of programs that can help you discover your talents, grow as person, improve as a professional, or all three.

The more skills you develop and the more hang-ups you eliminate, the more effective you'll be in a business environment (and everywhere else in life too). Make a habit of improving yourself and you automatically create opportunities to enhance your career, boost your income, and expand your enjoyment of everyday life.

FAST TRACK CHALLENGE:

Engage in one activity designed to challenge your comfort zone between now and the end of the week. Pick something that simultaneous thrills and terrifies you. If nothing comes immediately to mind, consider skydiving, public speaking, or calling an old flame (so long as you're single, of course). Whatever you choose, take action NOW and make sure it happens.

PRESENTING LIKE A PROFESSIONAL

"Take advantage of every opportunity to practice your com-
munication skills so that when important occasions arise,
you will have the gift, the style, the sharpness, the clarity,
and the emotions to affect other people."

Jim Rohn

ombetence in day-to-day duties is a baseline expectation for all
working professionals. There's room for significant variation in the
quality with which ordinary tasks are completed, but this is only one
of the places where Fast Trackers differentiate themselves from the competition. Presentation skills, interpersonal relationships, and attitude are where
they really tend to shine.

Of these, the best of the best universally focus on their ability to communicate in a professional and competent manner. They learn how to present in
front of audiences, articulate important business concepts, and sway opinions
through the power of speech.

The value of great presentation skills transcends the boundaries of industry,
occupation, gender, race, and age. A highly competent speaker has an advantage
over a less polished counterpart in almost every field of endeavor, and will often
outpace those with greater talent, education, and experience in the race for new
jobs and promotion opportunities. The ability to inspire, impress, and influence
an audience in critical situations (such as interviews, presentations, sales calls,
and board meetings) is among the most valued in the business world.

At the same time, the number of people who are able to make a truly competent presentation is tiny compared to the total number of professionals in the working world. Those who possess this ability are in a unique position to accelerate their career and reap personal rewards. Fortunately, this isn't a talent reserved for the rich and powerful. It's something that ANYONE can develop and improve.

In addition to speaking in front of a mirror and/or video camera (as covered in Part II), a great way to get started is to join Toastmasters. For about $65 a year you get world-class training materials, access to weekly or bi-weekly meetings, professional feedback, great networking opportunities, and a completely safe venue in which to practice public speaking. At just over five bucks a month, Toastmaster's might just be the single best value in personal/professional development on the planet.

FAST TRACK CHALLENGE:

Write a brief synopsis of your background that highlights your education, training, and work experience, as well as one significant accomplishment. When you're done, practice delivering this synopsis in front of a mirror or video camera until you feel completely confident in your presentation skills.

Example: My name is Mike Junge, and for the past 10+ years I've worked as a recruiter, executive, and entrepreneur in the IT staffing industry. I received my Bachelors degree in Creative Writing from the University of Arizona, and started my career as an agency headhunter with the company that became known as Kforce.com. Although I've had a lot of great experiences in the recruiting industry, the one I'm most proud of is...

WORK WITH A MENTOR

"I absolutely believe that people, unless coached, never reach their maximum potential."

Bob Nardelli

⚜ ⚜ ⚜

E veryone who achieves peak performance does so with the assistance of a coach or mentor. Even those with exceptional natural talent require guidance to reach the top of their game, and this is as true for business professionals as it is for professional athletes. The need for competent coaching is universal, and Fast Trackers are unwilling to operate for an extended period without a qualified guide.

The words used to describe the individuals who provide such assistance may vary—advisor, strategist, expert, teacher, master, guru, mentor, muse, and coach are common in various fields—but the practical value of having a committed expert on your side is indisputable.

What makes someone qualified to be your mentor or coach? The equation is relatively simple: they are someone who has achieved something you want to achieve, gained a skill set you would like to acquire, holds a position you would like to attain, or can otherwise provide value in your personal quest for success. In short, **a mentor is someone from whom you can learn.**

GETTING FOCUSED

Finding the right resource is the key to the whole equation, and that requires something from you. Namely, it requires *knowing what you want.* There are countless people in the world who have achieved great things and coached others to do the same. You can learn and grow by working with any of them, but unless there is clarity about exactly what you want to achieve and where you're looking to go, you're probably wasting your time (and worse, theirs).

You used the first part of this book to create a vision for your life and career, as well as short and long-term goals. Take a few moments to review your notes from Part I and get reminded of what you're up to and where you're going. Once you've reconnected with your goals you can begin taking the next steps in finding a mentor or coach who can help along the way.

---Review your vision and goals from Part I---

Given your specific vision and goals for career, identify an area where you are looking to achieve growth in the immediate future. Narrow your list down to a single top priority, knowing that you can always come back and add more later. When you narrow your focus down to a single area of concentration and put all of your energy on it, your odds of success go way, way up. This is one of the hidden lessons in Napoleon Hill's *Think and Grow Rich.* Narrow your focus and expand your results.

Area of Focus:_____

Now think of two or three people who could potentially be mentors in that area. Working with someone who has succeeded in one of your areas of interest is the ideal situation. It gives you a chance not only to learn from ideas and theory, but also from observation, direct feedback, and personal interaction.

Potential Coaches/Mentors

1) _____

2) _____

3) _____

GETTING CONNECTED

Once you've identified a list of potential resources, the next step is to figure out what it's
going to take to elicit their help and support. If
the potential mentor happens to be a friend or
family member, the effort may be as simple as
picking up the phone and saying, "Hi, ____.
It's Mike. Listen, I've been really impressed
with your success in the business world and
would love the opportunity to learn from you.
Would you be willing to spend a little time
giving me some guidance and pointers?"

If you don't know the person it probably
won't work to jump into their life from way
out in left field and say, "Hi, I'm a big fan.
Would you be willing to mentor me?" You
could try that, but you'll have a much better
chance if you can find a way to get a personal
introduction (à la LinkedIn or via a recommendation from a friend). If a personal intro-

> ### WHEN GETTING A JOB IS THE FOCUS...
>
> Consider hiring a career coach. A career coach has specific domain expertise and is paid to provide unbiased guidance through the various stages of the job search and career growth process. If possible, hire via a personal recommendation, ideally from someone who has gotten great results.

duction isn't an option, it would be worthwhile to find a way to build rapport
in advance or offer some form of compensation in return for their time.

Compensation can come in many forms and doesn't have to be money (though
that often does work). If cash isn't a viable possibility, consider volunteering as an
intern, offering up your expertise in a different area, or providing an alternative
form of reward (e.g., a barter arrangement). To build rapport you could participate

in a common charity or cause, find ways to meet through a networking group, or connect online via a social or professional networking site. Any of those can work.

GIVING AND GETTING VALUE

Once you've connected with a coach or mentor, there are some simple things you can do to make sure everyone gets value from the relationship. The first is to do what the person asks of you. Listen to their advice and guidance. Demonstrate that you value the relationship by putting what they tell you into practice. Nothing expands a coaching relationship faster than a willing apprentice, and nothing shuts one down faster than a student who just won't listen. A mentor can only give as much as you're willing to accept, so take as much as you can and put it directly into action. That's what makes it worth their while to coach you.

At the same time, pay attention. You can learn a great deal by simply watching an expert at work. Notice what they do and how they do it. Observation is often just as useful as direct advice and guidance. Many top performers don't know why they're so much more successful than others, and even more struggle to put into words what makes them different. Paying attention allows you to pick up on the subtle habits and personality traits that set them apart and put them at the top of their game.

Finally, ask questions. Try to learn the "why" and "how" of their success as you work through the coaching process. Why do they do things the way they do? Why do they think the way they think? Why do they want the things they want? On what do they focus the majority of their energy and attention? Why do they (or their students) get better results than the other people around them? Mindset, motivation, thought process, and attitude are instrumental to success, so focus on these and you'll be well-positioned to get value from the coaching relationship.

FAST TRACK CHALLENGE:

Reach out to at least one person you identified earlier in this section and get started in a coach or mentor relationship as quickly as possible.

FINAL THOUGHTS

"Don't let the fear of the time it will take to accomplish something stand in the way of your doing it. The time will pass anyway; we might just as well put that passing time to the best possible use."

Earl Nightingale

⊛

Before this book draws to a close it seems appropriate to review a few of the key concepts presented in earlier pages - particularly the ones whose relevance will continue long after your job search is over. Getting hired is a beginning more than an ending, and you'll probably experience at least a few more along the road to retirement. If you want those beginnings to happen on your terms, the smart play is to continue thinking like someone whose next job search is just around the corner.

Start by creating your vision and goals. Give yourself the gift of purpose and direction, regardless of what your situation happens to be right now. No matter where you are or how things are going, it's a good idea to have your next target in sight.

Being strategic about the future shouldn't in any way diminish your commitment to employers in the present. To the contrary, loyalty and outstanding performance should be central to your long term career strategy. The best case scenario is to find a company you'd be happy to work for indefinitely and rack up promotion after promotion until you run the place.

Practically speaking, you work in a dynamic marketplace and should prepare accordingly. Even if you love your job today, it is far better to position yourself for a change that never happens than allow the whims of the economy or those of a particular employer to dictate your professional fate.

To that end, the effort to become an Opportunity Magnet will be central to your ongoing success. Chasing work is a laborious and painful process (though the right attitude helps), while being pursued by enthusiastic suitors is a lot more fun and far more fiscally rewarding.

At the end of the day, attraction power is what differentiates the average job seeker from an Opportunity Magnet, an ordinary person from a Purple Squirrel. The more easily your audience can find you and validate your value as a resource, the more likely they are to start chasing you down and offering you work. Getting to the point where that happens takes time, but the benefits of making that investment are enormous.

If you happen to be out of work now, don't be afraid to take a more aggressive approach and proactively go after the job market. Employment is power, and the faster you get back to work the better. Landing a job quickly might mean adjusting your expectations in the short term. That's ok. Do what you have to do land work, kick butt at whatever job you're given, and stay focused on achieving your longer term goals. Do your best with whatever you are given, and trust that the rest will work itself out.

The secret to searching for work in the internet age is to do it intelligently — not through grunt force effort. Instead of visiting dozens of job sites looking for relevant listings, use Job Posting Aggregators to search the entire web at the same time. Instead of blindly submitting your resume to a given company, spend a little extra time identifying an internal point of contact to whom you can direct your inquiry. Instead of grunting it out on your own, partner with friends, family, and recruiters who can help you find relevant openings and facilitate the interview process.

In job search, the goal is to be both efficient and effective. Saving time is great, but not if it's at the expense of results.

As you build your online presence, remember that your audience has to be able to find you. Employers use key words and phrases to rapidly identify relevant talent. This is true on search engines, job boards, networking sites, blogs, and community forums, so the fundamentals remain the same in every venue.

The right combination of words and phrases can help capture the attention of your audience and force them to look more closely at you as a prospective resource. A little research will enable you to identify what employers in your market are hunting for and empower you to build an honest resume that consistently attracts positive attention.

When it comes time to interview, the keys are preparation and relevance. Do pre-interview homework appropriate to your level of experience, and remember that it is equally important to "own" your own background and identify the goals of each individual interviewer. After all, it's your background, and they're the ones who will recommend hiring you (or not). Intelligent preparation sets you up to answer interview questions in a contextually relevant and useful way, and that's one of the keys to landing great offers and healthy compensation.

Once you've landed a new job it's all about getting on the Fast Track. That means exceeding expectations from the start and getting better for the duration of your tenure. Fast Trackers take intelligent initiative, proactively seek feedback, and go out of their way to listen to the needs of others. They build networks, engage in personal development, and focus on making a tangible difference for the people they serve.

A winner in the modern job market is a person who is happily employed and constantly pursued. That's where the magic happens, and if you stay on the right path, that's exactly where you're headed. The job and career of your dreams are waiting. Go out there and grab them.

7780898R00129

Made in the USA
San Bernardino, CA
16 January 2014